Crafting Your Company Strategy:

A Business Plan Template and Example

Contents

Foreword

I wrote this book with care and compassion about your business and your journey as an entrepreneur. If you are just starting your business, I understand how difficult and stressful it might be for you because I've been where you are now.

The advice in this book is based on my accumulated experience of running my own businesses, coaching over 1,000 entrepreneurs just like you, and questions and feedback from the millions of people who have benefited from my work over the years.

This book's goal is to make your journey as an entrepreneur an easier one by giving you direction and confidence. I wish you best of luck and hope that the book will contribute to your success.

PART 1:
PLANNING

Chapter 1:
Introduction To Business Planning

"Whether you think you can, or you think you can't, you are right."

-Henry Ford

1. What is a business plan?

I'll tell you two things a business plan is, and one it isn't.

A business plan can be a formal document you hand to some organization, investor, or keep for internal company use.

A business plan is also the strategy for how you will execute every part of your business. This doesn't have to be a written plan. You can plan your business strategy in your mind. What's important is that you have a *viable and quality plan of action* before you start your business, and not just plunge into a business blindly.

Now, let me tell you what a business plan isn't. Don't think about it as a prerequisite to starting a business like a homework assignment that must be completed and handed in before you can start. It also isn't something you have someone else create for you because you aren't sure how to write it. And it certainly shouldn't be your excuse to procrastinate on the actual work you need to do to start your business.

I like to define the business plan as a cohesive strategy for your business that you may plan in your mind or in a written document that covers each major component of your business, how those major components will work well with one another, and your plan for executing those strategies.

If you are not sure how to create an effective business plan and you are a first-time entrepreneur, learning *how* to plan your business is a very good first step. Learning empowers you long-term. You will be able to use what you learn about planning a business in your current business and every new idea in the future. As an entrepreneur, you must develop the habit of always learning and improving your skills and learning the skill of business planning should be high on a first-time entrepreneur's priority list.

It might also help to get coached on planning your business so you can learn faster by getting guidance from an experienced business person while you both work on your business plan together. But don't just pay someone to write a business plan for you just to feel good that you have it. You must understand why every detail of your plan is in place.

In an effort to make this book more helpful, as one of the extras in this book, I can provide feedback on your business idea or business plan. Since I can't read everyone's full business plan, please wait until you get further in the book and learn how to create the simple 3-sentence business plan. Send that to me and I'll be happy to give you feedback and suggestions.

2. When business plans are needed

There are two instances when you should write a business plan. The first is when some individual or organization that you want to work with specifically asks for it. The second is for yourself to help you organize your ideas.

Even if you don't need a formal business plan to give an investor, you should always go through a rigorous planning process for your own sake to create a good strategy for your business. In my opinion, that is the true value of business planning.

The process of thinking about and planning your business can help you catch and correct many mistakes before you start. It is much more expensive to realize that you are heading in the wrong direction after you start your business than during the planning stages. The value of business planning is to identify problems and fix them early, while it is still cheap to do so. As a rule of thumb, the later you find problems with your business, the more expensive and time consuming they will be to fix.

There are additional benefits to writing the business plan even if you don't plan to use it for raising money. The process of writing can help you think through strategies more easily than if the plans were just in your mind. Writing out your plan also gives you a central place that contains strategies that you and your partners can agree on. This will reduce misunderstandings among team members and facilitate discussions and brainstorming sessions. Another benefit of having a written plan is that you can send it out to gather feedback. Plus, if your plan is written, you will be able to use it for reference in case you forget any details.

3. What makes a good business plan

A good business plan isn't about the formatting, length, or using big, fancy words. While those things can add to your plan's professionalism, what matters above all else is the quality of your strategies.

If you are a first-time entrepreneur, it can be difficult to gauge the quality of your strategies because everything is new and confusing. Even experienced entrepreneurs can make mistakes. Everyone has blind spots and no one knows everything. Once you put aside your ego and embrace the idea that no matter how good your plan might be, it can always be improved, it will be easier to seek additional help to ensure that the strategies in your business plan are the best they can be.

If you are a first-time entrepreneur, it is wise to consult with someone who has experience and a proven track record in your industry. I am not suggesting that I should be your mentor since mentors should be experienced in the type of business you are starting. Later in the book we'll cover how to look for mentors and get expert feedback on your ideas.

Seeking mentorship or help is not a sign of weakness. It is a sign of wisdom and humility. No one should do this alone. Someone with experience can easily spot a blunder that may waste a lot of time and money if it isn't caught early.

When I look back at my entrepreneurship journey, some of my biggest mistakes could have been prevented if an experienced mentor steered me toward a better direction before I embarked on making big errors.

4. Role of planning in your entrepreneurship journey

Later in this book, we'll examine takeaways from top entrepreneurship literature; theory and wisdom gathered over the last 100 years. For now, I'll give you a few of those takeaways with which to approach this book.

Planning is necessary. But over-planning can lead to stagnation and procrastination. The goal of planning is confidence, decisiveness, and action, not more planning. An ideal plan has natural strategies for you to begin executing sooner rather than later. Execution is key. That is why the second part of this book helps you execute as effectively as possible.

From my experience in business on my own and in coaching entrepreneurs, I observe that starting already puts you ahead of 50% of everyone out there because most people never start.

As you work on your business, with persistence, you will become better than 60%, 70%, and eventually even 80% of everyone out there. That is well above average, but it isn't enough. You don't win by beating the average. You win by being the best. After you start, continuous work and experience in your field will make you better than 90% of competition, and eventually you will win big when you begin to execute at the top 1-2% level. The goal of the second part of this book is to help you get there.

5. What is a business model

A simple definition of a business model is how every component of your business works on its own and in relation to every other component of your business.

Let's unwrap that definition. A business is made up of many separate components like marketing, creating and improving the product, finances, employees, consumer relationships, inventory management, and much more. What is important in a business model is that its different components are not just great individually, but work well together. This might sound simple, but it is difficult to make everything fit just right because the details are ever-changing and you have to constantly adapt while ensuring that the overall plan is still tightly put together.

Neither your business model nor your business plan are static. They evolve over time and you must constantly refine them. The stronger your business model is during the planning phase, the better your business will be positioned to succeed.

As businesses get started, grow, and evolve, the management team must constantly evaluate every component of the business model to ensure that they continue to work well together.

6. My personal journey into business planning

If you are reading this book, you are likely in the early stages of your entrepreneurship journey. First of all, congratulations on starting. I hope you find success and fulfillment.

I understand some of the emotions and experiences you might be going through. Starting your first business is confusing, daunting, and stressful. There is financial stress, pressure from friends and family, and then there is the stress from self-doubt, isn't there? Until we achieve success, we have no idea when it will come, whether it will ever come, and how long we will struggle before it finally arrives.

Starting a business can feel like a freefall and the scariest thing for a person in freefall is not knowing how long the freefall will continue, and whether the landing will be a hard or a smooth one.

When I started my first company, I had no business experience. My education is in Computer Science. Everything in entrepreneurship was new and confusing. I felt like everyone knew more than I did. Everyone had opinions as to what I should do with my business. In hindsight, it is easy to see that those opinionated people were also mostly beginners, but their ideas seemed good at the time because I didn't know better.

And since I had no way to evaluate ideas or strategies, I plowed ahead without much planning.

Even if I did the business planning on my own, what could I really plan? I had no way to tell whether one strategy was better than another. All my plans were made at a novice level.

As you can guess, my initial businesses were disasters that crashed and burned. Ouch!

My success came much later, but from years of struggle and misery of failure arose a passion to ensure that other entrepreneurs get the kind of help I never had. This led me to create many resources to support entrepreneurs, a coaching practice, and eventually a number of business books including this one.

After helping many entrepreneurs, I realized that simplicity and focus in planning is key, and that you can describe the core of any business in just three sentences. That's why I created the 3-sentence business plan. It is a perfect place to begin your business planning journey. So let's dive right in.

Chapter 2:
Introducing The 3-Sentence Business Plan To Help You Start With The Simplest Possible Business Plan

"If you can't explain it to a six year old, you don't understand it yourself."

-Albert Einstein

"Life is really simple, but we insist on making it complicated."

-Confucius

1. 3-sentence business plan introduction

Almost all companies have three components they can't do without: a product or service, promotion, and financial sustainability.

Here is the 3-sentence business plan template:

<u>Product:</u> What is the product and who is the target audience?

<u>Marketing</u>: How will you promote the product?

<u>Finances</u>: How will you generate revenue?

Narrowing things down to the bare essentials will help you focus on identifying the optimal business strategies.

Throughout this book, we'll plan a wide variety of businesses. Let's start by going over two examples to solidify this concept.

2. 3-sentence business plan example for a technology product

Let's start with a 3-sentence business plan for a mobile app that assists people in writing a business plan.

This is an established app I built years ago. I am using it as an example because I can use the wisdom of hindsight and behind the scenes information to give you deeper insights about this business.

<u>Product</u>: Mobile app to help entrepreneurs write a business plan

<u>Marketing</u>: App store search, publicity, social sharing, and ads

<u>Finances</u>: Revenue will come from subscriptions and upsells of educational business products and coaching

It is that simple to outline the core of a business with just a few lines. The sentences don't necessarily have to be full grammatical sentences either. The app idea is explained in one line and the handful of *most effective* marketing and monetization strategies are also expressed in one sentence each.

3. 3-sentence business plan example for a lawn care business

Now let's take a look at a 3-sentence business plan example for a lawn care business. It is a traditional business that most people have encountered before.

<u>Product</u>: Residential lawn care for residents of xx city?

<u>Marketing</u>: Google search, Yelp.com, YellowPages.com, and other local business listing websites, referrals, classifieds, business cards & business networking, fliers, paying for ads

<u>Finances</u>: We will focus on long-term customer retention to cover customer

acquisition costs, charge customers more than the cost of labor and expenses, and keep the difference

See how simple it can be to express almost an entire strategy for a business? Now let's try an exercise to help you create your 3-sentence business plan that we will later expand into a 1-page business plan and then a full-length business plan.

4. An exercise for your business

Try to address the questions that pertain to your situation. 99% of the time, it is possible to condense it to just three sentences.

Product:

- What is the product or service?
- What benefit does it provide and to whom?
- Can you make it inexpensively and of high quality?
- What form will it take? Website? App? Brick and mortar business?

Marketing:

- Identify a few of the most effective marketing strategies to promote your business

Finances:

- What are the major sources of revenue?
- How will this happen profitably?
- When will you achieve financial sustainability?
- Do you need to raise money for this? How much?

Answer the questions that apply to your situation and you will have completed your 3-sentence business plan, and in the next chapter you will expand this into a 1-page plan.

Chapter 3:
Next Baby Step In Business Plan Complexity: 1-Page Business Plan

"Progress lies not in enhancing what is, but in advancing toward what will be."

-Khalil Gibran

1. 1-page business plan introduction

While the 3-sentence business plan is my invention to help you ease into business planning, the 1-page business plan is something you can begin to use. Investors or potential partners might ask for it to quickly familiarize themselves with your business.

Let's begin expanding our 3-sentence business plans into a 1-page business plans.

2. 1-page business plan example for a technology product

Title: Mobile app 1-page business plan

Product:

The product is a series of mobile apps on Android and iOS. The apps will help people create a business plan and aid them in starting a business.

The apps will help people plan their businesses in these 3 ways:

- Offer tools to help entrepreneurs create a business plan and save their plans on the app

- Provide educational tutorials to guide beginners

- Offer live help on the app

Marketing:

The marketing of these apps will be through mobile app store search, publicity, our website, and social sharing from people inviting business partners to help plan their businesses on the apps.

Since the bulk of downloads for most apps comes from app store search, that is where we will concentrate.

Monetization:

We will make money by up-selling educational business products, coaching, and in-app purchases.

Profitability:

Since the app has minimal costs to build and maintain it, almost all revenue is immediate profit.

Target customer:

Young entrepreneurs, first-time entrepreneurs, people who need help, guidance, and tools to plan a business.

Size of opportunity:

These apps can reach over 1,000,000 people per year at their full potential.

Founding team:

Alex Genadinik is the founder and the main engineer. This is a single founder business. I'll outsource design work, but can handle all the other tasks.

Previous funding:

None

Costs:

Under $2,000 per year for initial design and ongoing outsourcing.

3. Analysis of a 1-page business plan example for a technology product

With this 1-page business plan for a mobile app we took a baby step and expanded the 3-sentence business plan for a mobile app from the previous chapter into a 1-page plan.

All it took to go from three sentences to one page is a slight elaboration on the three core components of a business plan, and the addition of secondary sections like team, costs, and previous funding.

We also added sections that describe the target customer and the overall size of the opportunity. You should never start a business without a deep understanding of your target customer and your competitive business landscape. I left out the competition section, but that may also be added. These sections are important in a business plan of this length and longer.

4. 1-page business plan example for a traditional business

Title: Lawn Care Business Plan

NOTE: the statistics used are not real. They are made up for the sake of creating this example.

Executive Summary

Bob's Lawn Care operates within San Francisco, California, and services the area within a 30 mile radius of the city.

Product Overview

The company offers residential lawn care, landscaping, and yard work. The main focus is on providing affluent residential lawn care services.

Current Progress of the Business

The company was founded in April 2012. Since then we have opened a small office and hired a salesperson and two full-time employees.

We currently have 25 residential accounts that we service on a monthly basis.

Our current growth is approximately 5 residential accounts per month while losing about one per month.

Target Market

Our focus is the high-end residential market. Our research shows that there are 120,000 single family homes in the area we target.

Market Size

From industry research, we know that approximately 40% of affluent homes hire lawn care companies to maintain their lawns. That leaves us with a market size of about 48,000 residential homes.

Additionally, there are 1,000,000 non-affluent homes in the area, 5% of which hire lawn care companies. This adds another 50,000 homes to the target market.

Additionally, there are 10,000 apartment buildings, 80% of which use lawn care companies.

That brings our total market size to 106,000 residences. The average account size brings in an annual $5,000 per account, which makes our total market opportunity: 106,000 residences multiplied by $5,000 = $530,000,000 per year.

Competition

We compete with numerous lawn care and landscaping companies such as John's Lawn Care and Pete's Lawn Care. We are different from most of our competition in the quality of work we provide.

We provide higher quality work at higher prices, which enables us to target more affluent consumers. This will lead to higher margins. Due to our higher quality of service, we will also retain customers for longer periods of time.

Financials

Our current annual revenue from our 25 accounts is $125,000 per year. Our major annual costs are:

1) Staff salaries for the 4 current employees (including CEO): $120,000

2) Office space: $20,000

3) Equipment and vehicles: $30,000

4) Additional, miscellaneous and one time costs: $10,000

Total costs are $180,000, which brings us to a net loss of $55,000 per year.

Marketing And Sales

We are currently marketing via 3 methods:

1) Direct sales and reaching out to potential clients

2) Building a professional referral network with other local service providers

3) Online advertising via our website, searches and listings on other local-service websites

Current Team

Bob, CEO and founder, has over 20 years experience in the lawn care industry and previously ran a successful lawn care company in Los Angeles, which he sold when he moved to San Francisco.

The rest of the team is comprised of one sales person and two employees who provide the actual lawn care services.

What We Are Looking For

We are looking for a business loan of $300,000 in order to fund our growth via marketing and sales for the next two years and help us get to 500 accounts, which will result in annual revenue of approximately $2.5 million.

5. Analysis of a 1-page business plan example for a traditional business

You might argue that this 1-page business plan was a little bit longer than a page and you are correct. I expanded on our 1-page app business plan in order to take another step in complexity as we work up to writing the full business plan.

The only thing I did differently here is dig a little deeper into the financials of this business. I elaborated on the costs, target customer, revenue, and how this business would become profitable.

Now let's move forward and learn how to write a full business plan. Since we already have the 1-page business plan, this step is not as scary as it would have been if we were starting from scratch.

Chapter 4:
How To Write A Business Plan

"If you fail to plan, you plan to fail."

- Benjamin Franklin

The sections below are the parts of a typical business plan.

Each section has:

- Theoretical tips on how to write that section
- Practical suggestions on how to approach that part of the business strategy for the real world execution of your business
- An example excerpt of that section from a full business plan
- Analysis of that excerpt

This way you get a combination of theoretical and practical advice on how to approach each section of the business plan, have a template to work from, and have an example and its analysis for reference.

In my opinion, the biggest value is the practical advice on how to approach each of the issues in the real world. When you start your business, execution will be the biggest factor in making your business successful.

Even if you don't want the practical advice and just want to learn to write a business plan, this chapter works as a template with an example and an explanation for how to write each section.

NOTE: Since the business plan is broken up through the sections of this chapter, if you want to see the full business plan in its entirety, you can find it in the appendix after the last chapter of this book.

1. Executive summary

The executive summary should be one or two paragraphs. It is an introduction to your business plan. It explains the problem your business is solving. It can also contain your company's mission statement. Use the executive summary to prepare the reader for what you will cover in the rest of your business plan. You should briefly explain what your product is, but do not go into too much detail about the product or other components of your business. You will have a chance to get into details in subsequent sections.

Quick note: some industries have another meaning for the term "executive summary," which is a very shortened business plan that is only about 1-2 pages. Don't get these confused.

Example of an executive summary from a business plan for my mobile app:

I am building a full 4-app mobile app series on Android and iPhone that will help people plan their business and support them through planning, starting, and growing their business.

This is a revolutionary new take on mobile apps where the apps become the business coach, guide for entrepreneurs, and give entrepreneurs the support they need to succeed.

The reason there are 4 apps in the series is because each app covers one of the biggest challenges for entrepreneurs:

- *Business idea stage*
- *Business planning stage*
- *Fundraising guide*
- *Marketing*

The comprehensive scope of the apps positions them to be the dominant mobile apps for entrepreneurs.

Analysis of the executive summary from the business plan for a mobile app:

My goal with this executive summary was to clearly explain what the product was, and to make the business sound intriguing and unique to the reader to make them want to continue reading. I emphasized the uniqueness of this project and how it can become a go-to tool for entrepreneurs. That signals to the reader that this will be a big opportunity.

2. Your product or service

This is the section where you should be more precise about your product. Explain your company's product or service. Is it a website? A physical store or service? A widget or a mobile app? What is special and different about it?

Explain why this product or service should exist, and why it is needed. Does it entertain? Does it make someone feel better? Does it solve a problem for someone? Does it teach something? What is the benefit of this product or service?

It may sound like a silly way to pose the question, but surprisingly many companies create a product or service that is not really needed, which causes difficulties when trying to sell, promote, or get people to use it.

Additionally, if your product or service is only needed a little bit, and doesn't necessarily solve a huge pain point or provide great value, it may be difficult to get people to pay for it.

Lastly, but very importantly, unless your product or service is very self-explanatory, explain how your product achieves what it promises to achieve. Don't leave that question unanswered or vague.

Example of the product section of a business plan for a mobile app:

These are mobile apps for Android and iOS. There are 4 apps on Android and 4 apps on iOS. The apps help people plan, start, and grow their business.

The reason there are 4 apps on each platform is that each of the 4 apps helps entrepreneurs with a specific stage of starting a business. The 4 apps cover:

1) Business ideas

2) Business planning

3) Fundraising

4) Marketing

Each of the 4 apps helps new businesses in these 4 ways:

1) Software tool to help people plan and save their plans right on the app. People will be able to create small business plans, fundraising plans, and marketing plans on the app.

2) Ability to plan parts of their business with partners and invite their whole team to collaborate via the app.

3) Tutorials to teach the entrepreneurs about the business stage they are in: business ideas, business planning, marketing, and raising money.

4) Live business coaching and advice provided by an expert. In most cases, until the app has sufficiently grown and to ensure quality of help, the coaching will be provided via text chat on the app by the founder, Alex Genadinik.

<u>Analysis of the product section of a business plan for a mobile app:</u>

My goal for this section of the business plan was to clearly explain what the products are and how they help people. I tried to make the product sound intriguing or different to make the product compelling. I also wanted to paint the picture that these apps have potential to be dominant or best within their product category.

Even if your product is a commodity service like lawn care, you can still make it interesting and unique by highlighting something compelling about it. Maybe you design the lawns using cutting edge modern art principles, have award winning customer service, or use organic grass products. These are just examples to show that any product can have something unique about it - no matter how commoditized it might be.

3. What stage of the business are you in?

Are you in the idea stage? Or have you started your business and maybe you have a prototype of your product? Or do you already have some revenue and a team, and your focus is on growth?

Do not get into too many specifics here. Simply establish where you are in the process of building the company to provide context for the reader.

It makes a big difference if your company is just being planned, or if it is already established and has achieved some level of success. The further you are in starting and growing your business, the more credibility your strategies garner.

Even though it is advantageous to be further along, don't be shy if you are just at the idea stage. It is OK to be at *any* stage, even the planning or the idea stage. Every successful company has at some point been in planning stages. Just be honest about where you are in the process.

Example of the business stage section of a business plan for a mobile app:

- Founded in 2012

- 50-100% growth year over year in first 3 years

- 25% growth last year due to saturation on Android and lack of growth on iOS

- Next year focusing on iOS growth

- Over 1,000,000 downloads

- Revenue last year: $125,000 (*Fictitious due to privacy*)

Analysis of the business stage section of a business plan for a mobile app:

In my version of this section, I was able to outline a few years of progress since these apps are live. That gives the reader a sense of the trajectory of the business in addition to the company's current status.

This section will be much simpler for you to write if you are just starting your business. All you will have to say is that you are either in the planning stages, or mention some initial accomplishments you've achieved after starting.

If you are at the beginning stages of your business, the more you can say that you did, the better you will look. This is because many people do not end up actually starting their business. So the more you can set yourself apart and show accomplishments and progress, the better.

Even if you have not started, you can talk about your market research, customer development (I'll explain what this is in a later chapter), or anything else you've done. Anything you actually accomplished will boost your credibility.

4. Your target market

It is easy and tempting to think that everyone can use your product, but that would be a mistake. Of course, you would like and encourage everyone to be your customer, but there are some people for whom your product will be a better fit. Identifying who those people are and focusing on that particular consumer base will also help you better target your marketing efforts and form your product or service.

Especially in the beginning, try to understand who will be the ideal customers for your product. Once you identify your target consumer, market your business effectively to them and get them to love your product, then you can expand to other types of consumers.

You can identify potential customers in three ways: demographics, psychographics, and geolocation.

Demographics are things like age, sex, income, education level, marital and parental status, car or home ownership, and many other measurable attributes.

Psychographics are people's attributes that can't be measured precisely, but are still important. These include desires, wants, hopes, fears, hobbies, interests, insecurities, mental blocks, common emotions they are prone to, and even things like confusion and delusion.

Geolocation targeting is self-explanatory. Some businesses draw clients from local areas and some businesses draw clients globally. A local liquor store draws most of its customers from the surrounding five block area while an average restaurant draws most of its customers from a slightly larger surrounding neighborhood. A handyman business can attract customers from anywhere in a city or a few neighboring towns because the handyman is able to travel there. An online business has a wider reach, sometimes attracting clients globally, although some countries tend to be far better target markets because they are wealthier and usually have more people with disposable incomes, or speak a language that is best suited to consume your product.

Let me give you a concrete example of how I identified a target market for my business plan app.

I'll explain what the geographic targeting, demographics, and psychographics are for the users of this app so that you can see my thought process for identifying them.

First let's cover the geographic targeting. The app is an English-only app so the best countries for this app are ones with a large base of English language speakers and Android users. These countries are USA, Canada, UK, Australia, South Africa, India, Indonesia, Malaysia, and a few other large countries that have large populations because even if a small percentage of people in those countries speak English, that would still make for a significant user base of English language speakers.

The demographics for this app are a little more nuanced. Most people who use apps are generally younger. Most entrepreneurs tend to be younger. Most of the users for this app are under 30 years old, and often under 25 years old. They are typically not wealthy since usually younger people are less affluent than older people, and entrepreneurs are not known to be wealthy when they first start out either. The users for this app are almost always first time entrepreneurs, single, and often still in college, just out of college, or even in high school.

The psychographics are where things get interesting. What are the app users like as people? What do they need and want in life? Over time, I have gotten to know my app users pretty well. Very often they aren't necessarily interested in starting a business as much as they just need to make some money. Usually that happens to people when they are in somewhat dire and stressful life circumstances. They need advice and direction because they usually have very little support in their business ventures or careers, and are generally thankful when the app provides them with some support. Usually the types of businesses that people on my apps try to start are not too technical. Most of the businesses being planned on the app are different kinds of local services or other traditional businesses.

By combining the geolocation, demographics, and psychographics, we can understand a lot about the average app user. Once we have a deep understanding of our target customers, we can create a product that pleases them, and we can better understand how to promote our product to reach people who are in our target market.

WHAT NOT TO WRITE IN THE TARGET MARKET SECTION: Don't write something like "everyone" or "all women" or "all men", or "all people in some country or city". You have to show a much deeper understanding of your target consumer and their consumption behavior.

Understanding your consumer makes it easier and cheaper to reach them in large volume with targeted marketing and advertising. It also makes it easier to create a product that better satisfies their needs, and is used in a manner that is convenient to them (important for product adoption and customer retention). It also helps you better understand your market size, which enables you to make more accurate financial estimates.

Point to realize: Narrowing down your target market to some specific group is not the same thing as limiting the potential of your opportunity. Narrowing down is the process of identifying your *ideal* customers.

Another consideration is your addressable market vs. overall market.

A subset of your market are people who are more likely to become your customers.

The total addressable market is the entire market which your business services. The target market for your start-up is the subset of the total market that your start-up is in.

If, for example, you are opening a fine dining restaurant, the overall market for people who visit restaurants is probably everyone in your city. But your target market is much narrower. The market you can realistically target is only people who like to eat the kind of cuisine served in your restaurant, people who can afford to eat out, and who live within a few mile radius from your restaurant. Since in this example we are discussing a fine dining restaurant, the target demographic may also be over 30 or 40 years old.

Here is another example. The total United States shoe market is in the billions of dollars per year. But if you made a shoe that is a slipper for men, you could only sell that to a portion of men in the United States.

It might be *tempting* to say that your target market is all men because there is nothing preventing all men from wearing slippers. But it would not be correct to say that your target market is all men. Many men hate wearing slippers, and it can be difficult to force kids and teens to wear slippers. Some men 18-45 years old might not like wearing slippers because they might make them feel like a grandfather. Plus, some people prefer to walk around their homes barefoot. Older men tend to wear slippers at home, but as a demographic, they statistically shop less often. It turns out that older people who would like your product the most, belong to a demographic that spends the least. And that is not a great business situation.

The deeper you understand spending and behavior of different consumer groups, the better you will be able to estimate who you can sell to, and identify a target market that can be advantageous to pursue.

Additionally, if you said that the target market for slippers was all men, and if you tried to market the slippers to all men, that would result in quite a bit of wasted money, time, and effort since not *all* men wear slippers. Instead of saying that your target market is all men, you may make older men your target market, promote it in places they shop, and make the style and feel specifically tailored to their preferences.

Example of the target market section of a business plan for a mobile app:

The target market are first-time entrepreneurs who need help with topics like business ideas, business planning, marketing, and fundraising.

Demographics:

- *Largely under 35 years old (app users are usually younger)*

- *35% US, 10% India, 5% UK, 5% Canada, 5% South Africa, 4% Australia, 4% Malaysia, 3% Indonesia, the remaining 29% are in rest of the world, largely concentrated in the developing world since for many people there the smartphone is the only computing device they own.*

- *Low income*

- *Low education*

- *Not married*

- *No children*

Psychographics:

- *Don't necessarily need to start a business, just need to make money one way or another*

- *Largely low tech businesses*

- *Typically not the Silicon Valley start-up types*

- *Under financial stress and pressure*

- *Low confidence in business, maybe told by others not to do business*

- *Little family support*

- *No ability to make in-app purchases with a credit card due to being in the developing world. PayPal may be okay for some.*

- *Need a solution fast*

- *Have limited funds*

- *Prefer free*

Analysis of the target market section of a business plan for a mobile app:

It is important to emphasize that while you can get demographic data from market research firms and analytics software, to understand the psychographics of your customers you must be "nose deep" in their business. Find as many ways to talk to them as possible to understand their needs. By offering free help to my app users early on (I don't do that anymore), I got invaluable insight into what my customers needed, and was able to create a product that satisfied them. Finding ways to talk to current and potential clients will give you great insight about what they need, which will help you create a more useful product for them that you can more easily promote.

5. Your target market size

This is the total dollar amount of your company's industry. Some markets are multi-billion dollar markets. Some markets total tens or hundreds of millions of dollars. You have to show that you understand your market and its size.

If you are building a company that sells a niche product, your market size may be small, but if you are selling computers or cars, your market size is in the tens or hundreds of billions of dollars, and is obviously very large.

This section reassures the reader that you have done due diligence and understand the business environment in which you are operating.

WHAT NOT TO WRITE IN THIS SECTION: Do not provide vague approximations and write something like "huge, very big, millions, or billions." You must research and know the statistics of your industry. You have to be as specific as possible with the dollar amount of your market size. The closer you get to the actual dollar amount, the better.

After you've noted the overall market size, narrow it down to your specific target market, which is a subset of the total market.

Example of the market size section of a business plan for a mobile app:

The full potential for my apps will be reached when they dominate search and recommendation algorithms on both Android and iOS.

Just by dominating in search, these apps can reach approximately 1,000,000 people per year.

Once the apps are widely recognized, they can get big publicity from industry websites, magazines, and by being featured in the Apple App Store and the Google Play store. That would result in 100,000-300,000 additional downloads per year.

An average download generates $1.00 of revenue, which means that at its peak, these apps will generate $1,100,000 to $1,300,000 per year.

(Reminder: The financial data in this example is fictitious. Actual financial data is private.)

<u>Analysis of the market size section of a business plan for a mobile app:</u>

The challenge I faced when writing this section was that there is no research on the total market size for business apps. I had to make an educated guess about the full potential of my apps based on data I already had. The only metric that was possible to get was to look at download numbers of comparable apps.

6. Marketing plan: How will you market to your target users?

The marketing plan is one of the most important sections of a business plan. It was one of our three core components in the 3-sentence business plan.

There are many ways to promote a product or service, but not all marketing techniques work for all companies. Your marketing plan must contain the most effective marketing strategies you will use to consistently reach your target market and convert them to clients at a scale required for your business to succeed.

If your marketing plan does not contain viable and effective strategies, you may spend your time and money making misguided marketing efforts, which might result in wasted funds, effort, and many months of work without getting clients. Needless to say that many businesses don't recover from such errors and fail precisely due to having an ineffective marketing plan.

COMMON MISTAKE AND WHAT NOT TO SAY: If your marketing plan reads something like "I will promote my business by posting on Instagram, Facebook, Twitter, and handing out flyers and business cards" then my initial guess would be that you are on your way to making a very common mistake. This strategy is commonly used by novice entrepreneurs and first-time marketers, not because it's the best way to promote their unique business, but because they don't know any better. This is a big red flag that marks inexperienced marketers.

Later in this book, we'll go over the most common marketing strategies for common types of businesses. For now, just understand that your marketing strategies should be in sync with how your potential clients naturally discover your product or service.

If an investor or an experienced business person reads your business plan, they will put emphasis on the marketing plan because they understand that if you don't know the best ways to promote your business, there is no business. A common way investors spot inexperienced entrepreneurs is when their plans don't include an effective marketing plan.

Example of the marketing plan section of a business plan for a mobile app:

The marketing of these apps will be through:

- *Mobile app store search (Apple App Store and Google Play Store)*
- *Publicity and PR*
- *Social sharing from people inviting business partners to help plan their businesses on the apps*
- *My website Problemio.com*
- *Google search*
- *YouTube channel*
- *Podcast*
- *Facebook, Instagram, and AdWords Ads*
- *Ads on the Android and Apple app stores*

Since for most apps, the bulk of downloads comes from Android and Apple app store searches, that is where I will concentrate.

Analysis of the marketing plan section of a business plan for a mobile app:

My apps have gotten 95% of their downloads from app store searches. Another 4.9% of the downloads came from promoting them through various publicity and PR sources, social sharing, my YouTube channel, and my website.

I didn't try to create a podcast or use many other marketing strategies to promote my apps because secondary and tertiary marketing strategies tend to have a steep drop in their effectiveness. It is better to double down on the most effective marketing strategies to ensure that you execute them to your best ability than chase ineffective strategies.

This marketing plan is effective because its strategies work for most types of apps. If you've never promoted anything before, and aren't sure which strategies will be best to promote your business, get an experienced professional to help with your marketing strategy before you start your business.

7. Revenue model

In this section you must outline how and when you will generate revenue. How many revenue streams will you have? What will be your strongest revenue stream?

There is quite a bit of confusion around terms like business model, revenue model, and revenue stream. They often get mixed up. The term business model is often incorrectly used to express how your business generates revenue. As we covered earlier, a business model is something greater. A business model takes all the components of your business into account and evaluates how they work with one another. The revenue model is just a part of the business model, and a revenue model can contain one or more revenue streams.

Now let's go over some of the most common revenue streams and examine when and how they should be applied to your overall revenue model.

THE AD REVENUE STREAM

The ad revenue stream is the simplest revenue stream. All you do is create an ad, publish it on your website, billboard, or any other property, and you are set. But the truth is that your customers hate ads, and ignore them as much as possible. That makes ads so ineffective that they can only make a reasonable amount of money if the website, billboard, or other media on which they are placed gets a very high volume of views. And the per view revenue is typically atrociously low.

On the web, the most common place to get ads that you can place on your website is Google's AdSense program:

http://www.google.com/adsense

For most sites, AdSense earns somewhere from $5.00-$10.00 per 1,000 page views. A thousand page views is the common unit of measurement for ads. It is denoted by CPM.

If a typical CPM (cost per thousand views) is $5, then you need 10,000 views to make $50. To make $500, you need 100,000 page views. And to make $5,000 - which is getting close to the vicinity of a middle class monthly salary for one person in the United States - you need to generate one million page views, which is extremely difficult for most websites.

If you decide to monetize your business with ads, your site will need to attract millions of people for you to be able to make any real money and grow your business. What you can do to increase your revenue potential is to think of another revenue stream that can work together with your ad revenue stream to improve results or replace it entirely.

A common mistake in choosing a revenue model is having a mismatch of business type to revenue model.

To be effective, just like with the case of the marketing plan, the revenue strategy must reflect the reality of the business.

For example, the ad revenue stream needs many views to generate a reasonable income. If you don't have a high-traffic website or business, the ad revenue stream might not be ideal for the situation.

AFFILIATE REVENUE STREAM

The affiliate revenue stream is a popular one, especially on the web. An affiliate is a reseller of products or services provided by another company. Online, the affiliate reseller promotes relevant products and collects sales commission.

An example of an affiliate is when my clients need project management software. Since I don't make such software myself, instead of recommending other software without being rewarded for it, I can become an affiliate reseller of this software for companies that create such software and collect a commission when I recommend it to my clients and they sign up.

This can work in conjunction with ads or separately.

If you get it working, selling affiliate products can make an order of magnitude more money than publishing ads because the commissions can be substantial depending on what you promote. But that is not a guarantee because it isn't easy to sell products. Pound for pound, selling affiliate products is more lucrative than publishing ads if you had to choose one over the other.

TRANSACTIONAL REVENUE STREAMS

A transactional revenue stream is one where you get paid directly in exchange for goods or services. This includes most kinds of commerce. Most traditional services also use the transactional revenue stream. For example, doctors' offices, cleaning businesses, restaurants, etc.

The transactional revenue stream is a very simple and direct way to get paid. Its strength is its simplicity and direct path to revenue. There is no need for publishing ads or referring people to other websites or businesses, and in many cases there is also no waiting. You often get paid immediately.

Usually there are two challenges for this kind of revenue stream. The first challenge is that people have to pay. Since they typically don't like to do that, they have to either really need what you are selling, or you would have to perfect your sales skills. The second challenge is that as soon as something can be sold for a profit, others jump on the opportunity and the business environment becomes crowded and competitive, making it difficult to promote the business effectively or bring in new customers in high volume.

Additionally, competition is often followed by price deterioration, which causes everyone to make less money. Consumers love this because they get more options at cheaper prices, but this is bad for your business because you make less money.

Nevertheless, if you can sell something, that is a great option. You just have to beat all your competition.

Many people don't think of themselves as being able to make a product, but I'd argue that you *are* able to make more kinds of products than you think.

There are many different kinds of products. There are written works like books and information products like online courses. There are arts and crafts that you can make at home and sell online. There are mobile apps or software products you can create on your own or by outsourcing. You can even use 3-D printing and create 3-D products that can be sold online. There are many different kinds of things you can make and sell. Imagination is the limit. Just think of your talents. I am sure you will be able to come up with something great. An idea for a product may not come to you today, but if you think about it, a good idea will come to you sooner than you might think. Once you can create something, there are likely many places online and offline where you can sell it.

SUBSCRIPTION-BASED REVENUE

This is a favorite of business owners. Not only does this mean recurring and somewhat predictable revenue, but it also means that revenue can accumulate every month as you grow your subscriber base.

If you can maintain a higher sign-up rate than your unsubscribe rate, you will have a beautiful revenue growth graph that is always up and to the right, with more subscribers and revenue each month.

Plus, the dirty little secret of subscription-based revenue is that many people simply don't unsubscribe because they are lazy or uncertain of whether they want to completely cut off the service. Think about how many people maintain their gym memberships, but have not been to the gym in months (or years, ouch!).

MAXIMIZING THE POTENTIAL OF ANY REVENUE STREAM YOU CHOOSE

There are three common ways to maximize the earnings from your revenue streams:

    1) Sell more to customers either immediately or over time

2) Charge more

3) Optimize the rate at which you get new paying customers

Let's explore each of these in more detail.

Think about how to extend the lifetime relationship you have with your customers. For example, when buying a car, does your relationship with the car dealer end there? It doesn't. The dealer encourages you to come in every six months to service your car which gets you into a habit of going back to that dealer. When it is time to buy your next car, you are likely going to consider buying from them again. Plus, any time you visit them, they can sell you add-ons such as car accessories, earning them additional revenue. Plus, if anything in the car breaks that isn't under warranty, there is a chance you might use their mechanic services or someone they refer you to while they collect a commission on that referral.

As another example, let's consider an example of a blog that makes money with ads. If you visit the blog once, they will have one chance to make money from you by showing you ads. If you never come back, they lose the chance to show you more ads. But if you like the blog and become a daily reader, they can show you ads 364 more times that year. That is an increase in earnings by a multiple of 364!

If you look at almost any established business, you will notice a way in which that business tries to extend the length of the relationships with its clients. Even my business does it. I structured it to be able to help entrepreneurs over the long-term, whether they are at the idea stage or the growth stage of their businesses. If a person has a business idea, I am able to offer business planning products and coaching, help with starting the business, website creation, and long-term marketing. Many clients have worked with me for years and I recommend that you begin thinking about how to create similar long-lasting customer relationships in your business.

Whether or not you are able to increase the duration of your relationship with your customers, think about how to charge more for your products or services. You can charge more by improving the quality of your offering and by targeting a more affluent market in which people can afford higher rates.

Lastly, always work to maximize new customer acquisition rate and the percentage of people who you convert from inquiries to paying clients. Let's take a look at how to optimize your sales funnel as a way to improve sales conversion.

A sales funnel is the series of steps a person goes through from first learning about your business to becoming a customer. Sales funnels come in many shapes and sizes and just about every business has one. Optimizing your sales funnel can mean the difference between life and death for a business because the more effective your sales funnel is at converting visitors to buyers the less money it takes to acquire each new customer, making your business more profitable.

When you are marketing your business, you probably send people to your website or a physical location. That initial point where you direct traffic is the top of your sales funnel. Once people get to the top of your sales funnel, you must have a clear path for those people to follow in order to purchase something or perform some action that you want them to perform.

The first step to improving your sales funnel is to measure everything.

If your business has a website, use web analytics software to measure and understand what those website visitors are doing. The most common free analytics software on the web is Google Analytics. You can sign up for it and start using it here:

http://www.google.com/analytics

If you are not familiar with web analytics, it would behoove you to familiarize yourself with it. It will help your business and it is an industry standard. If you don't use analytics software, you are literally "driving with your eyes closed" because you have no idea what people are doing on your website.

Web analytics will help you understand how many people visit your website and what they do on each page of your website. At each page of your site, you need those website visitors to go to the next step of your sales funnel. With analytics, you will be able to see whether people are taking the steps you need them to take or whether the funnel breaks down somewhere, causing them to quit and leave your website. Knowing what your website visitors are doing will allow you to make adjustments to get your visitors to successfully progress through the sales funnel.

You may be asking how you can increase the rate at which people move forward through the sales funnel. What you have to do is make the steps clear and have strong calls to action (usually a big button somewhere on the page) letting people know where they need to go.

Experiment with where on your site the calls to action are and what text should surround them so more website visitors make it all the way through your funnel. Also experiment with different page layouts to see what design and color schemes might give better results.

The best way to experiment is to use something called A/B testing. A/B testing is a technique in which you have two or more versions of a web page. You then drive people to those versions of the page and test which version generates a higher rate of desired behavior. The version of the page that works best is the one you keep on your site.

Another way to improve your sales funnel is to shorten it. You can create a single page optimized for a single action that you want people to take. That kind of a page is called a landing page because once you create that page, you can drive people to land on it. It typically produces satisfactory results because prior to driving people to it, you are able to extensively test its effectiveness using A/B testing, and only drive people to it once you are satisfied with its effectiveness.

Landing pages are a great tool to help you minimize the steps in your sales funnel and, therefore, increase conversion of website visitors to buyers. Less steps means fewer people veering off the desired path in your sales funnel.

<u>Example of the revenue plan section of a business plan for a mobile app:</u>

Note: the numbers here are fictitious due to privacy.

- In-app purchases of content
- In-app subscriptions to coaching
- Up-selling coaching services off the app
- Up-selling my books and online courses
- Selling affiliate products like website hosting for new businesses and

legal and accounting services

- Sponsors

Annual revenue:	$125,000
In-app purchases of content	$45,000
In-app subscriptions to coaching	$30,000
Up-selling coaching services off the app	$20,000
Up-selling books and online courses	$10,000
Services	$10,000
Sponsors	$10,000

Next year projected annual revenue: $161,000

In-app purchases of content	$60,000
In-app subscriptions to coaching	$40,000
Up-selling coaching services off the app	$25,000
Up-selling books and online courses	$12,000
Services	$12,000
Sponsors	$12,000

Analysis of the revenue plan section of a business plan for a mobile app:

Just like in the marketing plan section of the business plan where I identified the most effective marketing strategies for my industry and product, I've identified the top revenue sources for apps and chose the ones that would be the best fit for my unique app.

The lesson here is that you have to understand your industry, how comparative companies generate revenue, take into account the uniqueness of your situation, and come up with the most effective ways to monetize your customers and retain them long-term.

8. Financials

Before you start your business and as it grows, you must have a clear view of its overall financial picture.

There are three sections of a financial statement:

1) Cash Flow Statement

2) Income Statement

3) Balance Sheet

Maintaining a cash flow statement, income statement, and a balance sheet can help you keep track and have a better understanding of the overall financial picture of your business.

Large businesses typically have accountants who work on this section of the business plan, but if your business is small or you are just starting, you can create basic versions of these financial statements.

Let's start by creating your own cash flow statement. A cash flow statement for a new business is a glorified itemized list of ways cash (and cash equivalents) comes in and out of your business.

For new businesses, I recommend creating two such statements. The first statement is for the time period before you open your business, and the second statement will deal with cash flow after you open the business. Finances for these two periods are very different.

As an example, let's say that you are opening a restaurant in the United States. First, let's focus on the cash flow before the business is open.

Some (not all) of the cash flows *out* of the business are:

- Renting of the physical space

- Legal fees

- Business registration fees and other license fees

- Salaries of few early employees

- Remodeling of the space and furniture

- Food inventory

- Tools, machinery and supplies

The cash flows *into* the business will be from funding sources like investments, loans, grants, donations, etc.

Now let's focus on the cash flow statement after the business has started. Some (not all) of the cash flows out are:

- Monthly rent

- Employee salaries

- Utilities

- Liability insurance

- Ingredients for the food

- Marketing costs

The cash flows *into* the business are the different revenue streams like alcohol sales, food sales, and maybe catering.

The reason that creating this document is so important is that it gives you a clear sense of the financial picture for your business and enables you to make financial projections. It gives you a way to understand how much money you will need to start and run your business until you reach desired milestones which are often the break-even point and the point of profitability.

Creating a cash flow statement also helps you understand how much money to ask for when pitching investors. Depending on the type of business you have, you can ask for enough money to get you to a particular milestone or to get your business off the ground if cash is what you need. Aim to secure about 9-16 months of financial runway after the business has started.

Example of the cash flow statement of a business plan for a mobile app:

Note: A small business should monitor cash flows monthly. More established businesses often track cash flows on a quarterly basis (every 3 months), but in this case I made an annual statement.

Note two: Due to formatting issues across Kindle and paperback versions of this book, the financial items are listed one after another, but usually this is done in an accounting software or Excel spreadsheet.

Cash Flows In (fictitious):

In-app purchases	$20,000
Coaching sold through the app	$50,000
Ads	$10,000
Product sales through the app	$40,000

Subtotal: $120,000

Cash Flows Out (fictitious):

Outsourcing development	$2,000
Marketing costs	$1,000
Apple developer renewal	$100

Subtotal: $3,100

That was a basic cash flow statement. Your cash flow statement might have more line items, but the premise will be exactly the same.

Now let's take a look at the second of the important financial statements which is the income statement. Once you understand how to create a cash flow statement, the income statement is only a small step up in complexity from the cash flow statement.

The difference between the cash flow statement and the income statement is that the income statement has more types of items that are included. Some examples of additional types of items in the income statement are interest you might accrue, loans, stock transactions, donations, and depreciations.

To simplify things, think of the cash flow statement as an aid to understanding the operational financial health of your business while the income statement gives you a broader picture of your company's financial health.

If you are just starting out or planning for a small business, your cash flow statement and your income statement might be identical or look very similar.

Example of an income statement:

Cash Flows In (fictitious):

In-app purchases	$20,000
Coaching sold through the app	$50,000
Ads	$10,000
Product sales through the app	$40,000

Subtotal: $120,000

Cash Flows Out (fictitious):

Outsourcing development	$2,000

Marketing costs	$1,000
Apple developer renewal	$100
Loan interest payment	$1,000
Computer deprecation	$500
Donation	$500

Subtotal: $5,100

In this example of an income statement, I took our existing cash flow statement and added interest, deprecation and donations. In this particular case, this showed that the business is slightly less profitable than the cash flow statement showed because there are a couple of additional expenses.

The last of the three financial statements in a business plan is the balance sheet.

There are three things that go into your balance sheet:

- Assets - Cash and property owned by the business
- Liabilities - Money coming out of your business
- Equity - Assets minus liabilities

There are two types of assets: Current assets and fixed assets. Current assets are the cash your business has in the bank, accounts receivable (money owed to you), stocks your business owns, or anything you've paid in advance. Fixed assets are things like inventory you might have on hand, supplies you own, and intangible assets like intellectual property such as patents or trademarks.

Now let's talk about liabilities. Just like with assets, there are two types of liabilities: Current and fixed liabilities. Examples of current liabilities your company might have are payroll and other bills you have to pay. Examples of fixed liabilities are debt, bonds you owe, or even owed pension payments to employees.

Once you add up your assets and liabilities, it is simple to calculate the equity of the business. To get equity, you simply subtract the liabilities from assets.

Balance sheet *(fictitious)*

Assets:

Current assets:

Cash in the bank	$50,000
Coaching clients payments owed to me:	$3,000
Total:	$53,000

Fixed Assets:

Laptop:	$1,000
Office supplies and furniture:	$1,000
Trademark:	$500
Total:	$2,500

Liabilities:

- Outsourcing freelance tasks: $500

Equity: $55,500 - $500

Subtotal: $55,000

Now let's calculate the profit margin. The formula for profit margin is:

Profit Margin = Net Profit / Revenue

First, a few definitions:

- Gross Profit: Income remaining after accounting of goods sold
- Operating Profit: Subtracts additional costs of your business

Costs:

- Under $2,000 per year in outsourcing for design and development of features that need to be coded
- Under $1,000 per year for marketing costs
- After the apps are built, 5 hours of my time per month
- Profitability:
- In the fictitious finances of this business, that would be $123,000 annually since the only cost is design and minor outsourcing.

Operating Profit:

- Since my business has only minimal other costs, after taxes on $120,000 (minus cost of design AND marketing AND accounting), I make $65,000.

Net Profit:

- After I pay myself ($50,000 annually) the business profit is $15,000

Profit Margin:

Net profit / revenue: $15,000 / $125,000 = 0.12 = 12%

Note that if I paid myself less, my business would have been immediately more profitable and with a healthier margin:

Net profit / revenue: $35,000 / $125,000 = 0.28 = 28%

Net profit / revenue: $65,000/ $125,000 = 0.52 = 52%

9. Forecasting for future years/months

Before getting into forecasting, it is important to understand the difference between a financial statement and a forecast. A statement means the data in the document is from the past and forecast means that the data is estimated/projected future data.

Let's start by discussing how to create revenue and profit projections for an existing business. Later in this section, we'll go over how to create forecasts for a new business.

Revenue and profit forecasts are two very similar calculations with the only difference being that when you calculate profits, the revenue is offset by expenses.

It is important to acknowledge that when you make projections, you are dealing with the future and no matter how accurate you try to be, no one can predict the future with 100% certainty.

The first thing you do when working on a forecast is identify a time period you want to forecast. A time period can be 3 months, a year, or a few years. Once you define a time period, the next step is to identify all the ways in which money comes in and out of your business. You can do that very similarly to the way you made your income statement and your cash flow statement.

Some costs and revenue sources will be fixed and some will be variable. For example, if a long-term contract, (revenue or an expense) is a fixed cost or revenue. Marketing budgets or revenue from expansion into new niches would be a variable cost since it is hard to predict how much it would be month to month.

Next, add the fixed costs, variable costs, and revenue sources. Make sure you give yourself a range when calculating the variable costs as these costs can fluctuate.

Also look at your industry's and general economy trends as this can impact your forecast. Plus, consider whether your business has aggressive expansion plans. For example, if the past statements were based on one product but you are launching five new products, you might incur significantly higher costs or the new products might impact the existing ones.

Once you take the growth rates for previous months, quarters, (3-month spans) or years and adjust them to anticipate changing market conditions or business strategy, you can use the growth rates from the past to project future growth rates.

Now let's discuss how to make projections and forecasts for a business that has not been started. It is much harder to create an accurate forecast for a new business because there is no previous data on which to base projections. But some parts of the process are similar to forecasting for an established business. You also have to set a time period and instead of looking in the past for data, what you can do is anticipate costs and expenses. Those can be relatively easy to predict because you probably have an idea of the number of employees you will have, office space you will need to rent, and inventory you must purchase.

Revenue is harder to predict. To make a revenue projection, look at how companies similar to yours started. You can also ask industry experts what might be reasonable to expect and base your revenue projections on your competitor research, guidance of industry experts, and your own industry expertise.

And just like you would consider market conditions when creating forecasts for an existing business, you also have to do that when forecasting for a new business.

10. Unit economics overview

This section outlines the financial dynamics of each transaction, giving you insight into how profitable your business is on a per-transaction basis, which will help you assess operational efficiency and identify what needs to be improved.

For example, imagine selling a widget. You sell the widget for a certain price, but it takes you time and money to produce, market, and sell the widget, all while incurring costs such as paying your employees, rent, materials, and other bills.

You must figure out what it costs to put a widget into the customer's hands, and the price you will charge for the widget. That is a single transaction.

Once you dissect a single transaction this way, you can understand if it was profitable or lost money.

Your job is to figure out the number of widgets you need to sell in order to 1) break even financially on a month to month basis, 2) turn a profit, 3) finance further business growth or reach other business goals.

Also consider whether selling as many widgets as you need in order to meet your financial goals is viable through your available marketing channels and the size of your target market.

Example of the unit economics section of a business plan for a mobile app:

Since the product is a digital product and 99% of my marketing is from free sources, there is no cost of goods or marketing costs. Every download brings in *(fictitious)* $0.10 on average LTV (lifetime value of a customer).

The LTV per customer is on par with other apps. Most apps struggle to make significant money per customer and offset that by focusing on generating large volumes of downloads.

Since an app is a digital good and there is no cost to reproduce it like there is with physical products, any revenue is pure profit.

How I will extend the lifetime customer value (LTV)

- I use a "catalog" model to extend LTV by offering many upsells in the apps. I list all of my 20 books and 100+ online courses in the apps so when a person buys one, and they like it, they might buy a few more. Some rare individuals even buy my full catalog which immediately increases the revenue earned from them by thousands of percent compared to if they just purchased one product.

- I offer a subscription service on one of the apps. If a person subscribes for a year, that is 12 times more revenue than from a one-time purchase. This represents a 1200% increase in annual revenue. A two-year subscription represents a 2400% increase in revenue from the same customer, and so on as the subscription length grows.

- As one of the up-sells in the app, I offer long-term off-app business coaching which can generate thousands of dollars with the right client.

- I am working on improving LTV (lifetime customer value) by supporting the customers better, having them use the app longer by improving design, making features more useful and generally more beneficial. Longer engagement will boost monetization per customer.

- Email collection and email marketing to get people to re-engage with the app.

<u>Analysis of the unit economics section of a business plan for a mobile app:</u>

Since the apps are free and there is no immediate transaction when people download the apps, the goal is to retain the user long-term, make them a super-user to a point where they eventually warm up to the idea of paying for something on the apps. Once they warm up to the idea of engaging with paid options, those paid options are designed to maximize purchasing.

11. Current team

Provide a brief professional background of each member of your executive team, and discuss the current size of the team. Explain why each team member's experience is the right fit for this business. Bonus points if the team has worked together before and if members of the team have relevant experience in your industry. If you have great mentors or advisers, list them in this section as well.

<u>Example of the current team section of a business plan for a mobile app:</u>

This is a single founder business.

Alex Genadinik: 5+ years software engineering, 10+ years marketing, 5+ years product creation, successful entrepreneur.

<u>Analysis of the current team section of a business plan for a mobile app:</u>

This section is simple. Simply list the top members of your team, any board members, or notable advisors or mentors.

12. Your competition

It is important to understand the competitors in your business environment. Your competitors are to be respected, understood, and serve as examples if they are successful. You must understand why they are successful as well as their shortcomings. Where they fail may present an opportunity for your business to succeed by carving out a niche. Wherever your competition is strong is an opportunity to learn from them. You do not need to be better than your competitors at everything, but you do need to understand how your business will be different, and what part of the market you may satisfy better. You must have strategies for what you will do to compete against your competitors and come out on top long-term.

WHAT NOT TO DO: Don't obsess over your competitors or hyperfocus on their model. There will always be someone competing with you. Understand and learn from your competitors, but keep the focus on making your own business better. In the beginning, there are far more dangerous things than competition. New businesses are much more likely to fail from basic implosion if they do not offer a great product or service and sell it effectively.

Example of the competition section of a business plan for a mobile app:

- Other business plan templating apps. My apps are different in that they help entrepreneurs create higher quality business plans by educating entrepreneurs and discouraging an overreliance on templates that fill up the business plan with reused content.

- Gimmicky business plan apps that promise business plans in 5 minutes. Since my apps focus on the quality of the business plan and entrepreneur education, the business plans created with my apps are more effective.

- Pen and paper planners. Apps are more easily portable, offer cloud storage for natural backup, and can be used to plan a business with partners remotely.

- Business card apps, business news apps, productivity apps, and other big budget apps. These apps are not direct competitors, but I compete with them for similar searches in the Apple App Store and Google Play Store.

<u>Analysis of the competition section of a business plan for a mobile app:</u>

The right thing to do in this section is to list competitive products or companies. I didn't list any specific companies because I didn't want to give them extra promotion. Instead, I listed types of companies, products, or consumer behavior. In your business plan, list competitive companies, products, and user behaviors, and explain how you set yourself apart.

13. Previous investors and funding

Give an overview of how your business has been funded so far. Depending on who will be reading your business plan, you can add or remove sensitive information from this section (as well as other sensitive financial information throughout your business plan).

<u>Example of the funding section of a business plan for a mobile app:</u>

There is no previous funding. The apps were self-funded and created by Alex Genadinik, who retains 100% ownership.

<u>Analysis of the funding section of a business plan for a mobile app:</u>

This section is easy to write, but difficult to get right in the real world because it is stressful and difficult to create your business without necessary funding. But the problem with funding is that it is difficult to secure and even if you get it, you sometimes have to give away a part of your company ownership and with that, some of the decision making power. On the other hand, you don't want to go into personal debt to start a business.

In most cases, while it is understandably difficult to create a business without raising money, it is better to go as long as possible without outside funding. It leaves you in control of your business and debt free.

In the early stages of creating my apps, I did approach some investors.

Luckily they said no and I retained all the decision making power, collected all the revenue, and never had to make strategy decisions that investors would want to force on me in order to get a return on their investment.

14. What you are seeking with your plan

If you are handing the business plan to someone, you may want to add a section explaining why you are writing the business plan. Are you raising money? Are you hiring employees? Use this section as a closing to your business plan. If the reader got this far, they are likely interested. Let them know how they can get involved.

<u>Example of the "what I am looking for" section of a business plan for a mobile app:</u>

My company is looking to get into a start-up incubator and gain access to software development and app usability experts. That help will take the 4-app series to the next level in terms of quality and help it dominate in the app stores.

<u>Analysis of the "what I am looking for" section of a business plan for a mobile app:</u>

In my case, I don't need money. I need very high level and senior-level advice on important details of my apps, but most people create a business plan because they need funding. If you are looking to gain funding, list how much money you are looking to raise, and which milestone you are hoping to achieve with that funding.

15. Business plan appendix

If you have sensitive information in your business plan like private financial data, investor information or business secrets, you can place them in the appendix section of a business plan. The purpose of an appendix is to easily add and remove information depending on who you will be showing the business plan.

Example of the appendix section of a business plan for a mobile app:

My business plan example didn't have an appendix because I put all the financial information in the body of the business plan. In your case, you have the choice to move that information to this section.

Chapter 5:
More Complex Business Plan: Ecommerce

"Life is really simple, but we insist on making it complicated."

- Confucius

This chapter contains two business plans for the same company belonging to one of my clients. The first business plan is from before the company started, and the second business plan is from two years later after we took the company from near zero revenue to over $1,000,000 in annual revenue in the Ecommerce space.

The company name is *The Floor Guys*. The product is a bottle of grout cleaner called Grout-EEZ and their website is groutinfo.com, which you can browse for reference.

Disclaimer: I am not promoting this business. I chose this example because I can share real financial data and strategy insights to which I was privy and helped create.

1. Business plan for a real e-commerce business *before* it starts

Executive Summary

Cleaning the grout in bathrooms and kitchens is difficult because it requires hard scrubbing. There is currently no product on the market that cleans 100% of grout in different tile materials and most solutions don't clean very dirty grout effectively.

Jeff White, the creator of the Grout-EEZ grout cleaning product has been in the grout cleaning service industry for 20 years, physically cleaning grout in people's homes.

Recently, Jeff contracted a chemical company to create the perfect grout cleaning solution that can be bottled and sold. This business plan outlines the strategy to grow sales of the bottled grout cleaning solution, Grout-EEZ.

Product

Grout-EEZ cleans 95% of bathroom and tile grout without the need for hard scrubbing. It is the easiest to use and the most effective grout cleaner on the market.

Grout-EEZ comes in a single or a two-bottle package. The two-bottle package also includes a grout brush made specifically to clean grout lines.

Company progress

Grout-EEZ is a new cleaning product that just became available to the United States market.

Target market

The ideal customer is someone who cleans their kitchen and bathroom grout on their own, and is tired of ineffective cleaning solutions or solutions that make it difficult to scrub the grout.

Target demographics

- Home owner
- Middle class income
- 40-60 years old
- Primary cleaner of the house
- Home may contain kids or pets
- Deteriorating health or strength that may require easier grout cleaning option without scrubbing
- Female to male breakdown: 65% female and 35% male

Target psychographics

- Needs an easier grout cleaning solution
- Cares about cleanliness
- Will pay premium for ease of use, quality, and effectiveness

Market size

The market size for grout cleaners in United States is $100,000,000 per year. Since this is a niche cleaning product, there are no industry reports.

To research market size, we used:

1) JungleScout, which gives Amazon demand data

2) Google keyword tool, which shows Google search volume demand

3) 2200 Home Depot stores in US

4) 2155 Lowes stores in US

5) 5000+ Ace Hardware stores in US

6) Thousands of independent mom and pop hardware stores in US

According to JungleScout, the top earning grout cleaner makes $20k/month.

According to Google keyword tool, around 100,000 searches are made each month by people searching for various solutions to cleaning grout.

A website at the top of search results can expect to get 15% of clicks. A sales conversion rate of 2% is reasonable, which would result in 15,000 visits per month and 300 sales per month. 300 sales at $19.95 = $5,985.

The sales potential from two highest-priority marketing strategies online (Amazon and Google SEO), was $25,985/month as a best case scenario within a year. That would make the online market size approximately $310,000 per year.

In brick and mortar locations nationwide, we estimated that if an average location generates $25 in grout cleaner sales per day, then 10,000 locations generate approximately $91,250,000 per year in sales.

Online sales and hardware stores, combine to roughly a hundred million dollar per year market in United States.

Competition and how Grout-EEZ is different:

- DIY solutions with acid and vinegar
- Black Diamond grout cleaner
- Mildew and stain removers
- 100% organic solutions

The issue with DIY (Do It Yourself) or 100% organic solutions is that they are simply not strong enough to clean difficult grout. They only help with easy-to-clean stains. The same is true for generic mildew removers and the main competitor on the market, Black Diamond.

Many comparison tests show that Grout-EEZ is the most effective at cleaning difficult dirt from grout. It is also the easiest to use because it doesn't require hard scrubbing. These two points differentiate the product from all its competitors.

Marketing plan

The most effective ways to sell this product online are:

- Amazon (the biggest store online)
- Ranking the company website in Google search (SEO)
- Google Shopping and retargeting ads
- YouTube cleaning tutorials
- Customer support and retention via email and a Facebook group

The most effective ways to sell this product in brick and mortar stores are:

- Through brick and mortar stores like Home Depot, Walmart, Ace Hardware, and Lowes. It is difficult for a new product to get accepted in these stores so we'll create a strong brand online first and sell into these stores after.

Team and co-founders

Jeff White, Founder: Jeff has 20+ years of experience in the grout cleaning industry, where he went to people's homes to clean their bathroom and kitchen grout. Based on his experience, Jeff contracted a chemical company to create a grout cleaner that didn't require hard scrubbing and was effective and easy to use.

SWOT analysis

Strengths - highest quality cleaner on the market

Weaknesses - small team, low starting budget, competing against established competition, no marketing or sales expert on the team

Opportunity - commoditized and stagnating market ready for disruption

Threat - competitors may try to copy this type of a cleaner

Revenue streams

Amazon sales of Grout-EEZ at $19.95 per bottle.

Website sales of Grout-EEZ at $19.95 per bottle.

Amazon sales of the grout brush at $14.95 per grout brush.

Website sales of the grout brush at $14.95 per grout brush.

Amazon sales of the two-bottle plus free brush package at $39.95 per grout brush.

Website sales of the two-bottle plus free brush package at $14.95 per grout brush.

No short-term plans to expand to brick and mortar stores.

LTV (Lifetime Customer Value)

Most consumers first shop for a single bottle of the grout cleaner, which is $19.95.

During the initial transaction, we upsell the grout brush (additional $14.95) or the two bottle package which includes the brush for free ($39.95).

Long-term, since this is the best grout cleaning product on the market. Customers will come back when their bottles are empty. Most people clean their grout every few years and we expect 10% of our initial customers to become repeat buyers.

Cash flow statement prior to starting

Expenses:

- Product creation with a chemical company $5,000

- Package and label design $300

- Website creation $500

- Legal fees $300

- $500 inventory (100 bottle inventory at $5 to create each bottle)

Total expenses: $6,600

Revenue:

- N/A

Income statement

N/A for a business that has not started

Expected gross profit (revenue - cost of goods sold):

(This is the estimate before launching the product)

$20 sale - $5 to produce the bottle = $15 per bottle gross profit

Operating profit (including everything else like taxes, marketing, etc)

(This is the estimate before launching the product)

$20 sale - $5 to produce the bottle - $6 marketing per bottle including ads, website maintenance, or Amazon fee (if product is sold on Amazon) = $9 per bottle operating profit

Net income (profit left after all expenses have been subtracted from the revenue)

$20 - $11 = $9 per bottle

Profit margin (determines company profitability)

Net profit from previous section divided by net revenue

$9 / $20 = .45 meaning 45%

Pro forma (future) revenue forecasting

Forecasting revenue projections for a business that has not started is an estimate. However, to get more the most accurate projections, you can utilize projection tools on Amazon and through Google search such as:

1) JungleScout, which gives Amazon data

2) Google Keyword Tool, which shows Google search demand

According to JungleScout, the top earning grout cleaner made $20k/month.

According to Google keyword tool, around 100,000 searches were made by people searching for various solutions to cleaning grout.

A website at the top of Google search results can expect to get 15% of clicks which would result in 15,000 visits per month. Of those visits, you could estimate a reasonable sales conversion rate of 2%. This equates to 300 sales per month. 300 sales at $19.95 per sale is $5,985 per month and $71,820/year if we don't count up-sells.

If we combined the potential of two highest-priority marketing strategies, which were Amazon and Google SEO, it showed top revenue potential was $25,985/month as a best case scenario.

Balance sheet

Assets

Current assets: $0

Fixed assets: $500 of inventory

Intangible assets: $1000 for intellectual property on Grout-EEZ formula or trademarks

Total: $1,500

Liabilities

Current liabilities: $500 outstanding initial inventory order

Fixed liabilities: $0

Total: $500

Equity (Assets - Liabilities):

$1,500 - $500 = $1,000

2. Business plan for the same e-commerce business after $1,000,000 in annual revenue

Two years passed since the launch of the original Grout-EEZ product. The product has reached over $1,000,000 in annual revenue, and while that is a good achievement, much more growth and execution lies ahead.

What went well:

- Currently the top product in its niche on Amazon (where almost all the revenue comes from) generating over $100,000 per month in revenue and growing

- Great customer support and retention

- New products launched

What still needs work:

- The product now has to get into big retail chains like Home Depot

- The product doesn't rank #1 on Google search yet

- Newly launched products need marketing resources and time to reach their sales potential

UPDATED BUSINESS PLAN TWO YEARS LATER:

Executive Summary

The Grout-EEZ grout cleaning product is two years old. Grout-EEZ has proven to be the best grout cleaner on the market. It is the highest rated grout cleaner on Amazon and customers report better cleaning results compared to when they try other solutions. It is now the bestselling grout cleaner on Amazon.

This business plan will outline what's going well and the strategies to grow the product further.

The company has also come out with new product offerings.

Product line

1) Grout-EEZ cleans 95% of bathroom and tile grout without the need for hard scrubbing, and is the most effective grout cleaner on the market.

2) Grout brush helps scrub grout more easily and ergonomically.

3) Seal-EEZ helps protect the cleaned grout.

4) Stone-EEZ cleans stone tiles, which the original grout-EEZ product did not clean.

In research and development: A pet stain remover to help the company enter the lucrative pet cleaning market.

Company progress

Grout-EEZ has become the dominant grout cleaning product on Amazon. It has surpassed all our Amazon estimates, generating $112,000 in the most recent month.

Two years ago, the Amazon research tool JungleScout predicted maximum revenue of $20,000 in this niche, indicating that we have helped to expand the market inside Amazon. We still only sell it in the North American market.

Stone-EEZ just launched one month ago and data for it is inconclusive.

Current projects, research, and development:

1) Launch a pet cleaning product

2) Open a bigger warehouse for more inventory storage

3) Rank groutinfo.com online store #1 on Google search

Target market

The ideal customer is someone who cleans their kitchen and bathroom grout on their own and is tired of ineffective cleaning solutions or solutions that make it difficult to scrub the grout.

Target demographic

- Home owner
- Middle class income
- 40-60 years old
- Primary cleaner of the house
- Home may contain kids or pets
- Deteriorating health or strength that may require easier grout cleaning without scrubbing
- Female to male breakdown: 65% female and 35% male

Target psychographics

- Needs an easier grout cleaning solution
- Cares about cleanliness
- Will pay premium for ease of use, quality, and effectiveness

Market size

The market size for grout cleaners in the United States is estimated at $93,400,000 per year. Since this is a niche cleaning product, there are no industry reports. On Amazon where we will focus our sales, maximum annual sales for grout cleaning products is around $2,000,000 per year.

Google keyword tool, which tracks search volume demand for Google searches of a product, reveals that around 100,000 searches were made by people searching for various solutions to cleaning grout each month.

The leading website that appears first in Google search results can expect to get 15% of clicks. This would translate to about 15,000 website visits per month (100,000 searches x 15% click through rate). 2% of these click throughs are expected to convert to sales totaling 300 sales per month (15,000 visits x 2%) generating $5,985 in monthly revenue (300 sales x $19.95) or $72,000 per year.

This estimate is conservative because our lifetime customer value is higher than $19.95.

With higher conversion rates due to better branding and improving LTV, we can expect potential sales from Google searches to max out around: $150,000 per year. The revenue from other search engines like Yahoo and Bing is negligible.

The brick and mortar market consists of:

1) 2200 Home Depot stores in the US

2) 2155 Lowes stores in the US

3) 5000+ Ace Hardware stores in the US

4) Thousands of small hardware stores in the US

In brick and mortar locations nationwide, we estimated that if an average location generates $25 in grout cleaner sales per day, the over 10,000 locations generate approximately $91,250,000 per year in sales.

Combining online sales and brick and mortar store sales, the total market size is roughly a hundred million dollar per year market.

Amazon market: $2,000,000

Google search market: $150,000

Brick & mortar retail: $91,250,000

Total: Roughly $93,400,000 dollar annual market.

Competition and how Grout-EEZ is different

- DIY solutions with acid and vinegar

- Black Diamond grout cleaner

- Mildew and stain removers

- 100% organic solutions

DIY solutions and 100% organic solutions are simply not strong enough to clean difficult grout. They only help with easy to clean stains. The same is true for generic mildew removers and the main competitor on the market,

Black Diamond.

Grout-EEZ is the most effective at cleaning difficult dirt from grout, and that is what differentiates it from its competitors.

Marketing plan

The marketing plan for the coming year is:

- Continue to focus on Amazon

- Make every product a top seller on Amazon

- Make the groutinfo.com website rank #1 in Google search or all relevant keywords that generate customer traffic

- Increase ads that target people shopping for grout cleaning solutions

- Expand sales into large brick and mortar stores like Home Depot, Walmart, Lowes, and Ace Hardware

- Strengthen customer support and retention via email and a Facebook group

Team and co-founders

Jeff White, Founder: Jeff has 20+ years of experience in the grout cleaning service industry, where he went to people's homes to clean their bathroom and kitchen grout. Jeff worked with a chemical company to create a grout cleaner that didn't require hard scrubbing and was effective and easy to use.

The company has two employees for the following roles:

- Customer support

- Ads and other marketing

SWOT analysis

Strengths - highest quality cleaner on the market, dominant position on Amazon, cash on hand to fuel growth and hire staff

Weaknesses - still a relatively small team, only one major successful revenue stream

Opportunity - new product lines in different niches, higher Google ranking, and entry into big brick and mortar retail stores

Threat - large competitors may try to copy this type of a cleaner. Also a division of focus between different product lines and online vs. offline strategies may limit quality of execution of each strategy.

Revenue streams

Amazon sales of Grout-EEZ at $19.95 per bottle.

Website sales of Grout-EEZ at $19.95 per bottle.

Amazon sales of the grout brush at $14.95 per grout brush.

Website sales of the grout brush at $14.95 per grout brush.

Amazon sales of the Seal-EEZ (grout sealer) atf $39.95 per bottle.

Website sales of the Seal-EEZ at $39.95 per bottle.

Amazon sales of Stone-EEZ (stone tile cleaner) at $39.95 per bottle.

Website sales of Stone-EEZ at $39.95 per bottle.

Beginning work to expand to brick and mortar stores.

LTV (Lifetime Customer Value)

Most consumers first shop for a single bottle of the grout cleaner, which is $19.95 and some people buy the grout brush or the two-bottle package. Since this has proven to be the top grout cleaner on the market, there is a high reorder rate of 12%.

Average initial order size is $24.75 and reorder rate is 12%.

Cash flow statement (one-month snapshot shown here, but companies track this for every month)

Expenses per month:

- Product production: $25,000
- Storage warehouse: $700
- Website maintenance and updates: $100
- Ads: $2,000
- Staff salaries: $12,000
- R & D: $1,000

- Amazon commission: $30,000
- Taxes: $10,000

Total: $80,800

Revenue:

- $112,000 from Amazon

- $5,000 from website sales

Total: $117,000

Income statement

Expenses per month:

- Product Production: $25,000

- Amazon commission: $30,000

- Storage warehouse: $700

- Website maintenance and updates: $100

- Ads: $2,000

- Staff salaries: $12,000

- R & D: $1,000

- Taxes: $10,000

Total: $80,800

Revenue:

- $112,000 from Amazon

- $5,000 from website sales

Total: $117,000

Gross profit: (not including expenses other than product production):

$117,000 - $25,000 = $92,000

Operating profit (including everything else like taxes, marketing, etc):

$117,000 - $80,800 = $36,200

Profit margin (determines company profitability)

Net profit from previous section divided by net revenue.

$36,200 / $117,000 = .31 which is a 31% profit margin.

Pro forma revenue and forecasting:

The company has been growing at approximately 10% month over month, and we expect the same growth moving forward.

Balance sheet:

Assets

Current assets: $75,000

Fixed assets: $15,000

Intangible assets: $1,000

Total assets: $91,000

Liabilities

Current liabilities: $25,000

Fixed liabilities: $0

Total: $25,000

Equity

Assets - Liabilities: $91,000 - $25,000 = $66,000

3. Conclusion

Even though this company has achieved many great things during its two years in business, this business plan should illustrate that it still has a significant way to go. A million dollars in annual revenue can seem incredible, but as illustrated in the financials of this business plan, the profit, while still good is far less than the revenue due to expenses.

This company still has a substantial amount of work left to be done and room for expansion as it has not started to sell its products in retail locations and has not dominated Google search or sales through its website.

If you were to look at a 3-sentence business plan for this company, you'd notice that the foundational pieces of the plan are there. Here is my version of the 3-sentence business plan for this company:

- Product: Bottled grout cleaner

- Marketing: Amazon, Google search, Google ads, YouTube videos, product quality, customer support, long-term customer retention, brick and mortar stores

- Finances: 25-50% profit margin on each sale depending on reseller commissions

The first and third sentences are relatively basic. The second sentence - the marketing strategy - is the main challenge for this business. The better this company promotes its products, the better it will do.

The same is likely true for your business. The most effective strategies for your business are out there. Identify them, decide on them, execute at the top 1% level over the long-term, and success is yours.

Chapter 6:
Business Plans For Common Businesses

"You are absolutely unique, just like everyone else"

- Margaret Mead

This chapter focuses on common business that readers of this book tend to start. The chapter's aim is to ensure that you don't make the common errors made by most first-time entrepreneurs starting those businesses.

Before you start this chapter, please create or pull up your 3-sentence business plan. You can reference it while learning about common errors you may have made and immediately fix those errors and improve your plan. This will also help you see the before and after version of your plan so you can see how far it has come.

1. Commerce and e-commerce

A few types of businesses fall into this category. Commerce and e-commerce can include fashion designers creating great new clothes and needing to sell those clothes, people importing products and reselling them, people creating and selling digital products like ebooks or online courses, or people getting into affiliate marketing and trying to resell products made by other companies for a commission.

E-commerce is a great business because it is scalable, payment comes immediately after every transaction, many products are in strong global demand and thanks to the Internet, you are now able to meet that global demand with many great options for selling online.

There are a few major challenges that need to be overcome with such a business:

1) Identifying a great product in a profitable niche

2) Creating that product or having it created for you

3) Ability to scale production

4) Managing inventory

5) Selling the product effectively

Most products have a specific target market so you hardly have to wonder who the ideal customer is, and unless a product is in a hyper-niche, there is probably a big enough market for it. The more pressing issues are choosing the right product, niche, and generating sales.

During the sales process there are a few common mistakes. One common mistake made by first-time entrepreneurs is to start a commerce business and say, "I want to create a brand." Sure, that sounds great as a long-term strategy, but in the early phase, you need sales instead of branding.

Branding is awareness. When people are aware of something, they don't rush to buy. They rush to buy when they really want or need something. Your first priority should be going after people who are shopping and ready to buy *now*. That is usually done with direct sales channels rather than branding strategies.

When most people create their 3-sentence business plan for a commerce business, the product and finance sentences (sentences one and three) tend to be straightforward, but the second sentence - the marketing plan - is typically full of errors. It usually reads something like, "I will promote on Instagram, Facebook, ads, Shopify, and my website."

On the other hand, mine would specify: "I will promote my products through Amazon, search based platforms, long-tail SEO, Amazon ads and Google Shopping ads, customer support, and creating a personal brand in the product niche."

To understand the difference between the two marketing plans, you have to ask yourself a simple question: How do most people buy things online? Most people make the majority of their online purchases by searching Google,

Amazon, or other online stores, and despite all the hype, relatively few sales are made via Instagram and Facebook.

People who focus on direct sales channels and implement those strategies well, go on to create successful commerce businesses. Those who rely on social media to generate sales tend to struggle until they adjust their marketing strategy.

This principle isn't true 100% of the time. If you try hard enough, you can generate sales by standing with a sign on the street - but for most commerce businesses, the path to success is through direct sales channels where buyers typically discover your products after searching or already being in the middle of their shopping process.

2. Local business

Local businesses are the most common type of business planned with the help of this book. Local businesses are those businesses that serve customers within a specific radius. The radius can be anywhere from five city blocks for a corner store to sixty miles for a construction company that travels to do projects all over the local area.

Typical local businesses are brick and mortar stores, gyms, coffee shops, restaurants, nail and hair salons, home repair, residential and commercial cleaning, lawn care, dentist offices, doctors' offices, different types of therapy services, mechanic shops, community services, even religious services, and much more.

These are businesses that provide needed services. Since they are in demand, people search for these businesses when they need them.

Since people are searching for those services, the marketing plan (second sentence of your 3-sentence business plan) should include "local search, local ads, customer service, focus on customer retention, and passerby foot traffic" as first priority and "Instagram, Facebook, etc," as secondary priority even though most first-time entrepreneurs reverse the priority of these strategies.

A common challenge with such businesses is that they often require substantial funding to open a brick and mortar location in order to pay for rent and employee salaries. The need to raise substantial amounts of money is the most common reason such businesses don't get started. The financial section in the business plan will help you understand how much money you need to raise. Once you know how much money you need to raise, instead of pursuing just one fundraising strategy, it is best to combine a number of strategies like seeking investors, donations, grants, loans, saving money from your current job, getting a part-time job, holding fundraising events, or starting an abbreviated version of your business sooner rather than later and using that revenue to fund your bigger business.

3. Online service

Online services such as freelancing or starting an agency are popular. They can range from software development to marketing to design to copywriting and editing to coaching and much more. Plus, most of these services have a local component. Even though you can help people anywhere in the world, there are also people in your local area who are searching for your services. Local competition is far less challenging than competing for clients nationally or globally. Promoting your business locally will reduce the number of your competitors to only a handful.

The service industry is great because there is no inventory to manage and minimal costs to start. All you have to do is be able to provide the service and you are ready to start promoting them.

We just went over how to promote the local part of this business. But how do you get clients globally? Many people resort to brute-force outreach strategies, which work to a small degree because a small percentage of people will always respond. But many people don't like receiving unsolicited pitches and regard them as spam. Luckily, there are more effective marketing strategies that generate higher quality leads, and you guessed it, they involve search because when a person is searching, they are already interested in your services!

Unfortunately, ranking in Google search (SEO) is quite challenging for an online service business because there is so much competition. What works better is to make sure your profile is featured at the top of search results in freelancing sites where clients are actively searching for specific service providers. It isn't as competitive as ranking highly in Google search and while freelancing sites like Fiverr or UpWork are not without their challenges, they can bring many new clients, some of whom may become premium-paying clients.

Focus on providing an extremely high-quality service and make customer satisfaction your top priority. It will lead to long-term customer retention, which is one of the major keys to success for a service business.

Another way to get clients for this type of business is to become an influencer in your niche, which will get you wide recognition, authority, trust, and potential clients.

4. Influencer business

The Influencer business is a relatively new kind of business made possible by the democratization of media online. Prior to 1995, if you wanted to be on the radio, TV, or in newspapers, you had to go through gatekeepers in giant media companies. Today, all you have to do is make YouTube videos, start a podcast or blog, or create appealing Instagram content. If you can become good enough at your platform of choice, you can reach millions of people and be perceived as an influencer.

The business consists of creating content (writing, photos, video, or audio) consistently over a long period of time and being able to promote that content to a large audience. If you can create amazing content and be equally good at promoting it, you will grow a large following and become an influencer. Once you become an influencer, the ability to sell to your audience can help you grow any kind of business.

This is a great business because it is relatively easy to get started and you are investing in yourself. One challenge is that becoming an influencer is a branding move. There is no immediate revenue as with commerce or service businesses. The key to this business and the path to revenue for an influencer is to make yourself truly prominent and gain people's trust in you as an expert in your field. Once you do that, you can create a high-quality product of your own or promote any other business to your audience.

5. Platform business

A platform business is one that brings two kinds of people together. It can be buyers and sellers like on eBay, daters on a dating site, video creators and viewers on YouTube, dog owners and dog walkers on Rover, buyers and service providers on freelance sites, riders and drivers on Uber, or many other similar businesses.

These tend to be billion-dollar opportunities because they usually address universal needs. The challenge is starting and promoting them.

Since there are usually two parties involved (buyers and sellers) it is not only twice as hard to promote, but also the promotion has to occur rapidly and create a "critical mass" between the buyers and the sellers. If one group is thinly populated, the other group won't have a good experience and will be less likely to return to the site. If that happens, the original thinly populated group loses interest due to a lack of getting clients and will also quit the site.

Imagine trying to find a ride using Uber, opening the app and finding no cars. After trying it a few times, most people would give up and stop using the app. Then when drivers start driving, they would have no one to drive and also stop using the app, making the app useless for people looking for rides.

Since this type of business is marketing-intensive, it needs funding for rapid promotion. Most of these sites have to go through a professional fundraising process in order to secure enough capital to grow.

To solve the problem of generating "critical mass," such sites often begin by focusing on a niche in the market. The niche can be geographical or topical. Once they raise money and get a foothold in a niche market, they tend to be able to generate enough momentum, expand to other niches, and grow to become giant companies.

6. Innovative new products or businesses not mentioned

This chapter focuses only on the most common types of businesses and attempts to correct common mistakes. If the kind of business you are planning wasn't mentioned here, the rest of the book will help you plan for your situation and you can always get direct feedback on your 3-sentence business plan from me.

Chapter 7:
Business Planning Thought Process

"Intuition is a suspension of logic due to impatience."

- Rita Mae Brown

1. My thought process when evaluating new business ideas

This chapter will give you a backstage view of how I evaluate a new business idea by asking basic questions around risk and competition, growth potential, and overall business viability.

Keep in mind that I am not always right and this is just my own thought process. At times I can be a bit sarcastic and possibly a little too realistic so please bear with me.

2. Idea 1: Travel blog

My thought process:

Travel is a great industry, but you will be competing against many multi-billion dollar companies. To be successful, you must identify a smart niche or differentiation in the industry. Some examples can include travel to a specific country, type of location like national parks, or a particular kind of travel like backpacking or luxury travel. If the person with this business idea has not thought about the niche too deeply, I know that there isn't much of a business idea there at all. There should also be more depth and originality to the idea beyond just traveling and posting Instagram photos.

If the person telling me this idea did choose a compelling way to differentiate themselves, I proceed to think about how they will promote their business and whether they will be able to stand out. Will social media make sense to promote this business? Or will it be search engine marketing or YouTube or something else that will make for a great marketing strategy? If none of the marketing strategies feel natural or doable and instead feel like they might be too competitive, it is a red flag. If I see a red flag like that, I begin to brainstorm changes to the initial idea and further differentiation until I find a natural way to promote the business that can lead to a significant amount of traffic and clients.

The revenue model here does not concern me too much because the real challenge is to get high volume and engagement of traffic. Once you get the traffic, there are many proven ways to generate revenue in the travel industry.

3. Idea 2: New mobile app for photos, social media, or games

My thought process:

What do you think these kinds of apps all have in common? I'll give you a few seconds to think about it 1...2...3 OK, I hope you have your answer.

These app ideas are in competitive niches where their top competitors are multi-billion dollar businesses that have a loyal user following.

New apps in these crowded spaces have little chance of succeeding even if they are great apps. Competition is just too stiff.

New ideas in these niches can't get by without compelling differentiation. But even then, the niche might be too competitive to rise above the noise of the giants who dominate the space. Only get into this if it is a true passion of yours, you are prepared to spend years in this niche, and don't need immediate revenue. It is also a big plus if you are open to learning mobile app development so you don't have to lose money hiring people to develop the apps for you. It would allow you to experiment freely until you succeed.

4. Idea 3: Local lawn care business or other kinds of local services

My thought process:

I love local service businesses because all they have to do is provide a good service and beat out other local companies when it comes to marketing and promotion. It is much easier to out-market other local businesses similar to yours than businesses that compete nationwide or globally such as apps, travel, and other large industries.

The major concern is that many local businesses require substantial capital to open a brick and mortar location. I'd recommend focusing on either a fundraising strategy or a way to get started without needing to invest substantial capital.

5. Idea 4: A restaurant

My thought process:

This is one local service that is truly difficult to start and make successful. You need a substantial amount of money and countless licenses and permits just to launch. After you open, it can take months before you break even or turn a profit - if ever. Not to mention that you may be working 6 or 7 days a week and long hours. While I never try to discourage anyone, this is one business I urge people to research and think about extensively before opening.

Most people are saved from the mistake of starting a restaurant by the simple fact that they don't have the funds for it, and that makes them abandon the idea. But if you happen to be able to get the money to start a restaurant, be very careful, get a lot of coaching and guidance from a successful restaurant owner, or partner with someone who has extensive experience in this industry.

6. Idea 5: Affiliate marketing or making money online

My thought process:

These days I talk to at least one entrepreneur per week who has misconceptions about how easy it is to make money online with affiliate marketing.

The idea of making money online has all the promises of a nice and simple life where you work very little, sit back while collecting a paycheck, and quit your 9-5 job, and the daily commute. People who struggle at their 9-5 jobs or just want to do something more creative with their lives tend to fall for this and embark on businesses that promise to make money online. Affiliate marketing tends to be one of the most common online businesses because there is nearly no barrier to entry. It requires no skills, products, or services. It is predicated on reselling products or services made by other companies.

It is possible to make a good living by working online. I know this first hand because I do it myself. But I will be the first to say that for most people it takes A LOT of hard work and quite a bit of struggle. Don't be fooled by other online marketers promising you quick and easy money.

If it is too good to be true, it probably is.

My advice is to approach this business just like you would any other. Plan every aspect of your new online venture, make sure all parts of the strategy fit well with one another, and get quality and honest coaching in areas where you are inexperienced. Whatever you do, don't buy into get-rich strategies or expensive programs. They typically make someone else rich and put you in worse financial shape than you were when you started.

7. Idea 6: Any other new business idea

When you get a new business idea, immediately ask yourself:

- Am I interested in being in this business long-term? Do I have a natural curiosity for this industry? Will it fulfill or bore me?

- Can this product/service be built or delivered relatively inexpensively and quickly with enough quality?

- How can I market-test it inexpensively and quickly?

- Is the target demographic a lucrative one?

- Is there a big market for it?

- Does it solve a very big or desperate need?

- What are the natural marketing strategies?

- How long will the marketing take to begin working?

- Can this be done profitably?

- If this business succeeds, will it help me reach my financial goals?

- Is this the best way for me to reach my financial goals or are there better ways?

These questions size up the risk, viability of the business, the possibilities for growth, and whether it will be lucrative.

Chapter 8:
Business Planning Mistakes & Exercises To Overcome Them

"How much you can learn when you fail determines how far you will go into achieving your goals."

-- Roy Bennett

Perhaps the biggest mistake anyone can make is to think they are fine the way they are. From years of experience creating products and running businesses, I have developed a mantra for myself:

Everything can always be better.

If you are not making an effort to improve every aspect of your product and business, guess what? Your competitors are! The best advice that I give myself every day is to keep working on making myself better at everything I do. It isn't easy because it requires constant self-assessment, practice, and learning. Try to do everything you do well today, better tomorrow. The quality of your product or service will be a big factor in your success.

Make sure not to let your quest for perfection stop you from starting or launching. A good rule of thumb is to start and launch early and then consistently improve over time.

Now let's cover common entrepreneur mistakes that I hope you never make.

7. Mistake 1: Using planning to procrastinate

Don't use planning as an excuse to put off starting the work on your business.

Many people deliberately and perpetually remain in the planning and research phase while never starting. At some point you must start doing actual work.

Exercise to fix the mistake:

Give yourself a planning and research deadline. Create and maintain a daily to-do list of things you will actually do for your business after the planning deadline expires.

You should continue to plan, strategize, and research different aspects of your business after that deadline, but use that date as a point after which at least some of your effort will be actual work instead of planning.

8. Mistake 2: Avoiding financials

Many people find the finance section of the business plan confusing and put it off. You will need to face this at some point. It is much better to understand the financials of your business before you launch to avoid preventable mistakes.

Exercise to fix the mistake:

Start by making a cash flow statement. It was covered in the finance part of the business plan example, but let's go over it again to refresh your memory. Get a piece of paper or open an Excel spreadsheet. Use whatever you feel comfortable with. (Just recycle the paper once you are done with it!)

Once you have your piece of paper or Excel ready, simply make two columns. One column is for a list of ways that money comes into your business, and the other column is for ways that money comes out of your business. You can do this if your business has already started, or if you are just planning it. Try to think of as many items for each column as possible.

Over time, you will have items to add and remove from this list, and the dollar amounts will become more accurate.

The cash flow statement is the first simple way to get your finances organized and understand how much money you will need to raise before you start your business. This document is easy to create and maintain.

9. Mistake 3: Lack of readability

Whether you are planning to simply organize ideas send your plan to investors, it helps to have someone proofread your business plan for readability and provide feedback on your strategies.

Common readability issues are grammar mistakes, making your plan unnecessarily long or complex, incorrectly using complex or flowery language, or too many buzzwords. These types of errors can make a great plan appear unprofessional and turn off investors.

Your readers are human. Don't bore them. Don't confuse them and don't take more of their time than you have to. Keep your business plan flowing so your readers don't quit reading. The better they understand your plans the better the feedback they will provide you.

Exercise to fix the mistake:

Have your business plan proofread by people with two kinds of skills: business expertise and writing. First, get an expert in your field to look over your plan to spot strategy errors. If you can't find affordable business experts to give you feedback, the next best resource is your business peers. Don't forget that I offer to take a look at your 3-sentence business plan and give you feedback.

After your business strategies are set, if you need to send your business plan to investors, get the business plan proofread for grammatical errors. Re-read your business plan after you are done to see how it reads. Sometimes even reading it aloud helps.

I'll give you a pertinent example. This is the fifth major edition of this book and 19th internal revision. Despite so many rewrites, re-reads, and multiple editors, I still find many sentences and paragraphs that can be improved. The same will be true for your business plan. It can be boring to re-read your own plan, but doing so will make it much better.

10. Mistake 4: Outsourcing your business plan writing

I understand the temptation of having your business plan written for you since writing one can be confusing, frustrating, and - let's face it - pretty boring.

Think about what will happen if someone else who doesn't truly understand your business writes your business plan. It will be a generic, mostly copied and pasted plan that they probably got from some template. A good business plan should take your unique situation into account. Another person simply doesn't know all the details and will likely create nonspecific content. Plus, these services tend to be pricey so you might pay hundreds or thousands of dollars for a document you may never use.

Exercise to fix the mistake:

Write the business plan on your own, and get coaching or mentoring to help you with the difficult parts if you get stuck. A good coach or mentor can listen to your ideas, assist you in writing your business plan, and take many of the unique elements of your business into account when helping you create the best possible business plan.

Another benefit of having a mentor or business coach help you write your plan is that when they come across potential pitfalls, they can discuss those issues with you and teach you while improving the business strategy on the fly.

11. Mistake 5: Overly optimistic growth projections

Many new entrepreneurs talk my ear off (and the ears of everyone else they meet) about how great their idea is, how unique it is, and how it will revolutionize their industry and make them successful. It is great to dream big, but for most businesses that isn't how things play out. There is a lot of hardship before you can get to such a good place. A bit of realistic thinking is also needed.

Being excited is fantastic. It will give you early motivation and momentum. But it also causes people to be overly optimistic about their company's potential.

Exercise to fix the mistake:

I love the idea of dreaming big. I don't want to tell you not to do that. But here is an exercise that might help you find a good balance between dreaming big and grounding your decisions in reality.

Get feedback on your idea from business peers and experts. When you do, be sure to do more listening than talking. Don't be defensive if you hear something negative. Really listen and respectfully consider what people have to say. That dose of reality will balance your big dreams. You don't have to follow everyone's advice, but it is good to hear different opinions to gain a wide perspective of the situation.

It can be tedious and frustrating to seek and process feedback, but skipping this step can lead to many severe mistakes going unnoticed.

12. Mistake 6: Being all things to all people

When asked who their ideal customer is, many first-time entrepreneurs often say that their business will appeal to everyone. This is almost never the case. You must have a very specific kind of customer in mind in order to truly satisfy them with your product and reach them with your marketing.

Exercise to fix the mistake:

Talk to people who you think might be your customers and get their feedback on whether they need your product or service and whether they would buy it. Also understand their reasons for why or why not. This will help you develop a greater sense of who your potential customers truly are and who they are not.

When Paul Graham, founder of the Y-Combinator and one of today's most admired business leaders, mentors the hundreds of start-ups that come through his incubator, one of his common recommendations is to find the first hundred customers who will absolutely love your business rather than trying to please everyone early.

13. Mistake 7: Unfocused business ideas

An example of a focused business is a salon. An example of a salon strategy that lacks focus would be a salon that also sells massages, offers daycare, has an attached coffee shop, and miraculously helps the greater community.

Exercise to fix the mistake:

Focus on what your business is first and foremost. While the latter version of the salon sounds amazing and is fun to dream about, the reality is that extra complexity increases difficulty and chance of failure, and requires more money to open and operate. It is challenging enough to open a regular salon so keep things simple in the beginning and grow into your dream state later.

14. Mistake 8: Believing in your own greatness in a blinding fashion

While confidence is necessary, extreme overconfidence can be damaging and blinding. Few people have ever told me that they are bad at any task or that they don't think they will do a great job. But many people underperform when it comes to execution of their business. No one is perfect. We all must recognize our flaws through realistic self-assessment.

Exercise to fix the mistake:

Devote 5-10% of your work week to self-assessment and improvement of your skills and the quality of your business. For example, if your product design isn't ideal, work with a freelance designer. If you procrastinate, give some attention to forming healthier work habits. Be mindful of what's hurting you or your business and devote time to improve those weaknesses. You won't become great at everything, but fixing problem areas can often help you take a big step forward.

15. Mistake 9: Underestimating competition

Many first-time entrepreneurs have a tendency to say that they have no competitors or that they are better than their competition. But if you are just starting out, established competitors are probably better.

Exercise to fix the mistake:

Search Google for products similar to yours. It is surprising how many entrepreneurs don't actually do this or who Google something once, conveniently don't find anything noteworthy, and stop their competitor research. Make sure to Google extensively and look for competitors using different search terms.

Another way to find your competitors is by asking your potential customers which companies they use to solve the problem your business seeks to solve. Perhaps they'll shed light on who your competitors are.

Once you find your competitors, use their products to learn what they are doing well and what they aren't. Take what they are doing well as inspiration for your own business. If there is something they are not doing well, that can be your opportunity to outperform them.

16. Mistake 10: Falling for get-rich-quick schemes or oversimplified business ideas

Many people sell different business schemes that are either bogus or make it seem like it is easy to make money where in reality they just make it seem simple so that new entrepreneurs who don't know better buy into their training or coaching programs, but are ultimately left struggling.

While it is possible to make money online, few people are successful at it and I don't know anyone for whom it was easy. It often takes years of struggle and trial and error before gaining enough experience, knowledge, and skills to be successful.

Exercise to fix the mistake:

Build a network (sometimes called a mastermind) of entrepreneurs who may also be starting out. Your group can be as small as two and as big as ten people who would commit to meet on a regular basis, share insights, and assist one another. You can see what your fellow entrepreneurs are going through, and they might be able to help you spot poor decisions and correct them.

Don't buy into any expensive training programs, but do try to work on projects that require hustle and action rather than excessive spending. Learning by doing is one of the best ways to learn.

17. Bonus mistake: Choosing an unfulfilling or unprofitable niche

If you succeed, you will be in your industry for a long time so choosing something that fulfills you is a must. If you don't, you'll find yourself longing to get out of your business despite investing years of your life into it.

Bonus exercise:

We will spend the next chapter on how to choose the right niche. The business you choose is the foundation for everything you do moving forward, making picking the right niche extremely important.

Chapter 9:
Choosing The Right Business Niche And Improving Your Business Idea

"If everybody is doing it one way, there's a good chance you can find your niche by going exactly in the opposite direction."

- Sam Walton

1. What is a business niche?

A business niche is a subset of a market that a product or service might target in order to stand out or differentiate itself from the rest of the competition in that market.

2. Why do you need a business niche?

There are a few reasons to choose a business niche:

i. Your business idea will exist within some niche so focusing on identifying the right niche for you might help you narrow down good ideas.

ii. A niche helps you find an area within an industry where you can be competitive.

iii. Having a specialization within your industry helps people refer potential clients to you according to that specialization. For example, if you are a travel agent whose niche is Hawaii travel, your past clients and other travel agents may refer people to you who are planning Hawaii trips and need extra expert help. It doesn't limit you to serving to Hawaii travelers only, but it helps you be more attractive to those potential clients, and serve them better.

iv. It gives a manageable and realistic business landscape that you can dominate when starting out without having to spread yourself too thin.

v. It helps focus your business strategy and marketing efforts.

vi. It helps to differentiate your business from more established competitors in your industry. You may never have zero competitors, but finding a niche substantially cuts their number.

3. Looking outside vs. inside yourself

If you are looking for niche ideas, you can certainly look at popular magazines, book topics, TV shows, and other things in your daily life. There are plenty of large and lucrative industries that can give you inspiration for what your niche might be.

But it can be more powerful to first take a deep look inside yourself and examine your strengths and passions when searching for a good niche. Work from an understanding of who you are and what drives you and identify a business area that you want to get into because it will fulfill you as a human being.

Of course, once you get ideas, it is vital to evaluate your niche idea and business ideas in that niche using real world criteria that we cover throughout this book.

4. Further steps to finding a business niche

Not everyone gets fulfillment from their business, but it is great if you do because in most cases you will spend almost every day working on your business.

One challenge to choosing a fulfilling niche is that most people's passions fall into a few categories that are fun things like travel, music, sports, or relaxing. That hardly helps because it leaves many less fun industries that almost no one would get into if everyone just followed their passion. So let's broaden our niche requirement to: Have a strong interest in the industry or indirectly get fulfillment in which you decide to start your business. An example of getting indirect fulfillment is if your business puts food on the table for your family. That can be good enough because that will give you all the drive and motivation you'll need.

People say "follow your passion" because working in an area you are passionate about gives you intrinsic motivation to work harder, longer, and to forge forward during challenging times. Identify your strongest long-term motivators and start thinking about businesses within those areas.

After identifying your passions, strong interests, and motivations, the next step is to start evaluating your personal strengths. From all the things you are passionate about, what are you also strong in? These strengths will give you a natural advantage when running your company.

Some strengths can include ability to work alone, build and manage teams, network and leverage business connections, take rejection, creativity, fundraising, and many more.

Similarly, consider your previous work experience and education. Is there something within your work history or education that you can bring to the business as an advantage?

If you have industry experience, that is a major strength. In fact, if you don't have experience or industry knowledge, your first three to nine months of starting your business will be a huge learning curve and that might put you at a disadvantage.

Just as you should align your business idea with your strengths, you should also make sure to avoid ideas that expose your weaknesses. For example, if you aren't a people person, maybe don't start a customer-facing business. And if you don't know how to write software, trying to get into a technical business or a mobile app business would immediately put you at a disadvantage compared to engineers starting a similar business. Having a disadvantage does not mean that your business will necessarily fail. It just means that it will be more difficult to succeed.

The next point to consider when choosing an idea is whether you have to build a team or if you already have the necessary skills to do the work yourself. As your business grows, you will hire and outsource many parts of your business. But in the beginning, you or someone on your founding team should be able to do many of the necessary tasks. You simply won't have the resources to hire and outsource everything, nor should you at first. Have your hand on the pulse of as many parts of your business as possible in the beginning. It will help you understand the ins and outs of your business.

For example, if you want to make a mobile app, it makes a big difference if you can program the app on your own. App developers have an advantage over many people because they can make the app for free, whereas someone who doesn't know how to program would have to pay $10,000-$20,000 to get the app developed plus additional maintenance and improvement costs. That is a huge advantage for a person who is able to make apps right from the start.

Of course, there are levels of advantages. For instance, a well-funded start-up that has a whole team of engineers and designers who can make a much better app in a shorter amount of time than one engineer can.

Something else that might be helpful is if you already have a habit of dabbling in the area of interest of your business idea or niche. If you do, you won't have to force yourself to work on your business or rearrange your lifestyle. Habits help people stick with things. The power of habit is that it makes the task you are working on feel effortless and helps you to keep doing it longer. Whatever business you get into, having a related habit makes working on the business easier and increases your chances of success.

5. Niche size and competition

Finding a niche with the perfect balance of competition and size is another big challenge while planning. If you choose a niche that isn't competitive, but too small, the business you establish might not be able to get enough clients to bring sufficient revenue. But if you choose a niche that is too big, the competition may be too difficult to surpass.

There is a famous blog post on this issue by a well known and respected venture capitalist Mark Suster. The article is here:

http://www.bothsidesofthetable.com/2009/09/16/most-startups-should-be-deer-hunters/

To summarize the article, Mark talks about three kinds of markets you can take on. We can think of these as niches. He refers to these markets as an elephant, a deer, and a rabbit. A gigantic and competitive market is like an elephant. It is huge with potential for a big reward, but difficult to overcome. A market that is too tiny is like a rabbit. Even if you successfully hunt it, there isn't much meat on it. So a deer-sized niche is a perfect size. It is not too big to kill, and the reward is a good size.

Disclaimer: I am only using hunting as an analogy. I love animals and I do not hunt. But as an analogy, hunting makes sense.

When you are looking for your niche, aim for a deer-sized niche. It doesn't have to mean that you will always stay in this niche. Once you find success in any niche, you can always expand into bigger niches. However, you must start somewhere manageable.

Another point to consider when choosing a business niche or idea is realistic goals for your life. Your business should help you reach these goals. If your goals aren't astronomical, you may not have to go after the most competitive or challenging business ideas. That would make your entrepreneurship journey much easier and success more attainable.

Once you identify a business idea or a niche to pursue, you can begin to evaluate them further by applying some business planning rigor that we covered in this book. You can begin by considering how easy or difficult it will be to promote that business. Some businesses lend themselves well to certain types of marketing, but other businesses have fewer effective ways in which they can be promoted.

It does take an experienced marketer to correctly foresee what businesses are easy to promote and which are not. If you are not an experienced marketer, here are a few questions to ask yourself when evaluating how easy or difficult a business is to promote. Is the business something that people seek out when they need it, perhaps by searching on Google? Can it generate publicity from its uniqueness? Can it go viral from social sharing? Are there many competitors?

A similar evaluation process applies to monetization strategies so test how profitable the business might be. Some businesses have many natural ways in which they can generate revenue while others don't. Again, if you aren't sure, this is a good thing to get advice on from a coach or from someone experienced in these issues. You don't want to get into a business which will be difficult to promote or one that struggles to generate revenue.

It might seem like we are getting rid of many potentially good businesses. That is OK. We don't to settle on a mediocre business and when you are creating the foundational pieces of your business, the strategy must be put together well.

6. My early mistake when choosing a niche

When I started my first business, I had no idea what niche to get into, what made one business idea better than another, and how to evaluate them. There was no one to teach or advise me. There wasn't a book like this one, and there wasn't an online course I could learn from. When I was starting out there wasn't even YouTube! Yes, YouTube the company had not even been started yet. I guess I am old.

When you are new in business, everyone who knows at least a little bit about business seems like a great expert. At least that was how they seemed to me. One day, I met someone who professed to be a "business guy" and an "idea guy." Since I didn't know how to tell whether he was a true expert or not, I took his advice.

I have an education in Computer Science and I was working on my own software at that time, but I didn't know how to turn it into a business. He advised me to apply some of the technology I was working on to the fashion industry. I'll be honest with you: I have no knowledge or interest in fashion. Yet I took his advice and focused on shoes as my business niche. This was absolutely the wrong industry for me to get into.

Recall an earlier part of this book when I suggested to pursue a niche that you know something about. I didn't have that advice or insight when I started so I took this "business person's" advice and got into the fashion industry. That proved to be a big mistake.

Another mistake I made was not choosing a niche that was narrow enough. Going from all fashion to just shoes might seem like I narrowed things down, but shoes are still a multi-billion dollar industry that is far too vast with many multi-billion dollar competitors. Even if I narrowed all shoes to all sneakers, that would have still been too large of a niche. Sometimes you have to "niche down" much further than the original starting point. Even if I chose Jordan sneakers, since that is one of the most iconic sneaker brands, I might have found too much competition. Perhaps sneakers of players who played for a particular team would have been a good niche because that would have also created a natural marketing strategy, which would be to target fans of that specific team.

When I mentioned that I had chosen the shoe niche, I hope a red flag had gone off in your head screaming that the shoe industry is still a multi-billion dollar industry, not small enough as a starting niche, and that I should have niched down further. Unfortunately, such a red flag did not go off in my head, and I plowed into the shoe market without knowing anything about it.

That mistake led me to fumble around in the fashion industry for four months until the project failed. I learned a lot, but the outcome wasn't what I hoped for. I wish I understood then that I needed to get into a niche in which I had knowledge, passion, and experience. That is why I am sharing this with you here - so you don't make the same mistake because for me, this was a painful lesson to learn. Four months might not seem terrible, but when you are living something every day, and it fails, it's heartbreaking to experience. The more such errors I can help prevent for you, the better.

If you think I was done making mistakes with my niche choices, I wasn't. For my next business, I started a group hiking website similar to meetup.com but only for hiking where various hike leaders could use my website to run their groups and hikes. I can't say hiking was my passion, but I liked it and knew more about it than fashion.

One of the problems with this business was that I did not choose a niche for it other than just hiking, which made my marketing difficult from the beginning. I originally tried to start this business on a national level in the United States. But it was too difficult to get hike organizers to start using the website in different parts of the country. It diffused my focus on any specific area and competing nationally was too difficult early. To fix that, I shifted my niche to target a hyper-local area of Northern California, mainly San Francisco. But that was too small a niche to generate a significant income, especially considering that publishing ads was my original monetization strategy (another mistake).

I had to change direction again. This time the business turned into just me being the hike organizer and leading fun, themed hikes. Because the events were interesting and themed, I was able to charge for attendance. I was also able to get local publicity and many more attendees per hike than typical bland hikes. That business was able to bring in enough revenue to sustain me after I learned how to make the themed hikes flashy enough to bring in strong attendance and therefore revenue. It was okay as a tiny self-run business that supported its founder, but it was never going to become a multi-million dollar business that would fulfill my hopes for it because it was difficult to grow beyond just the hikes I organized. It did have some success, but not enough. Ultimately I had to move on.

Even though I was able to partially correct my niche errors, not only did it take time and postponed revenue, but changing course midway led to imperfect options that led to less than ideal outcomes. If I had planned my niche more accurately from the start, I wouldn't have had to struggle making those adjustments.

II had to experiment with many niches throughout my journey of those two early businesses, with none of the niche choices being ideal. No niche is ideal. Each niche has pros and cons, but we must ultimately choose one. Choosing it is often a combination of careful planning and ultimate decisiveness. Planning is a must, but if you wait to identify a perfect niche, you might wait too long and never get started. The ideal scenario is that planning should save you from making huge mistakes and you should expect to make some adjustments after you've started and hope that they do not have to be drastic.

7. How to brainstorm business ideas

It is great to get expert feedback about your business ideas, but you don't always have access to experts. If you can't get advice from an expert, you can still refine your initial idea by brainstorming with peers or on your own. In this section I'll share my favorite way to brainstorm business ideas. It does require patience and a thick skin, but it works.

When you get a business idea, ask tough questions about it to test it. The questions are nothing new. They are the typical business planning questions we keep coming back to in this book. The idea behind this brainstorming is to find flaws in the original idea so we can adjust the overall strategy to fix those flaws while keeping other original elements of the idea intact.

Sometimes when we adjust one part of the business strategy is adjusted, it misaligns other parts of the strategy and you have to go back and ask the questions all over again to make sure that the answers still make sense and the overall business model still holds up.

Here is a list of questions to ask:

- How will you promote the business?
- How will it make money?
- Does it target an affluent consumer base?
- How big is the market?
- Will you be able to compete in the current market?
- Will your founding team be able to bring this idea to market? What necessary skills is the founding team missing?

- How long will it realistically take to get this business to succeed? Do you have that amount of time to work on this idea?

- If not, how far will you have to niche down in order to make the idea simpler and more feasible?

- If you niche down and change strategy, will the questions above still have the same answers? Sometimes they don't, and strategy needs to be adjusted further.

The idea behind this brainstorming is to reject mediocre ideas until you find one that stands out that is much better than the one with which you started.

8. Have real conversations to get real feedback about your business

Once you've picked an idea and a niche and have analyzed it for any weaknesses, the next way to test it is by gathering feedback from different people. You can get feedback from friends and family, business peers, people who you think might be potential clients, industry professionals, and experts.

Friends and family are great because they are almost always available to you. The problem with getting business feedback from them is that they don't necessarily understand business or the industry you're in.

Business peers are good resources as well; however, there is a chance that these peers might also be beginner entrepreneurs and their insights might not be accurate.

Note of caution: When you ask people for advice, some people will say something like "that sounds great" or "that sounds awesome" in an effort to show their support. Don't fall for that as a positive sign. Those platitudes are too easy for people to say. Get into deeper conversations. Really explore their thoughts, pick their brain, and have a back and forth discussion. Just "nice" is not a sign of interest. In fact, it is a form of negative feedback. If your idea doesn't invoke a stronger reaction, it can be a sign that you've confused your listener or that the idea isn't as strong as you feel.

9. How to talk to industry experts

The best people to talk to about your business ideas are industry and business experts and potential customers. The challenge is that business experts are busy and difficult to get a hold of.

A way to easily talk to many industry experts is to join Facebook groups on the subject matter of your business or your industry. This won't work for all industries, but it will work in quite a few. There are large Facebook groups for just about any industry. You can join them and post questions there that many industry professionals will answer. You can try a similar approach with LinkedIn groups, but in the last few years Facebook groups have been taking over and becoming more popular, so try exploring professional Facebook groups first.

Personally, I have gotten help from people in such groups on many different topics including my online courses, books, YouTube channel, mobile apps, and much more. Most people in such groups are beginners, but if you have enough conversations there, you'll perk the interest of experts and get their advice as well.

The last group from whom to gather feedback about your business idea are potential customers. Identifying and reaching out to your potential customers depends on your industry and niche. Try to identify them and begin conversations with them early. You don't have to start selling to them, but get their thoughts on your ideas and whether they would be interested in buying the kind of product or service you are considering.

Chapter 10:
Planning Monetization Strategies

"Great companies are built on great products."

- Elon Musk

1. Benefits of planning for long-term use and engagement

Long-term clients are great because they tend to buy more, recommend your business to others, leave more positive reviews, and do other things that boost your business. But long-term clients don't just suddenly appear. They must be cultivated. In a savvy business, that cultivation begins at the planning stages.

One of the things to plan for is how to make your customers engage with your business long-term. A good example of this is how I am able to offer additional services to clients beyond just coaching. In almost any industry or business, the key to long-term customer retention is the value you give to your customers. When people have an amazing experience, they rush back for more. If they get just an okay experience, they typically don't.

As small business owners, we tend to obsess about getting new clients. But the ironic thing is that if our current clients love our product or service, it will be much easier to sell to existing clients than to find new ones. You must foster those relationships.

Plan for how you will position or create your product or service to make it a regularly consumed product or a product that becomes a part of people's daily life and habits. If you can accomplish that, you have a much stronger business case.

Consider the example of how food companies make many variations or flavors of their foods. If you like one flavor, you might want to try another, which for them means an immediate doubling of revenue. They also want you to love the food so you buy it every time you shop. If you buy some food repeatedly, the seller of that food will make 10,000%+ more revenue from you by using these two principles:

1) Make your product amazing

2) Have more things to sell to people who love your product

2. Long-term monetization strategies with their pros and cons

One of the most common and most effective long-term monetization strategies is the subscription model. The beauty of the subscription model is that a person can stay subscribed for many years even if they no longer use whatever they are subscribed to. They have to make an effort to unsubscribe. That five minute effort to unsubscribe creates a barrier for a person, which is amazing for you as a business owner. If people are not subscribed, the barrier is for them to pay, which is one of people's least favorite things.

The problem with subscriptions is that people are afraid to sign up for them precisely because they worry that they will forget to unsubscribe and keep getting billed. Luckily, there is a natural way to remove that consumer hesitation. That strategy is to sell consumable products. Consumable products are ones that people can consume and need again. Some examples of consumables are food, clothing, online credits, points in mobile app games, etc. You can even think of traditional services like lawn care as a consumable because people keep needing it over and over.

One way to make people consume your products on a regular basis is by getting people hooked on your product. A common example is in the app gaming industry. If you play a mobile app game and you can't beat a level, you might buy an in-app purchase that gives you extra lives to beat that level and get further in the game. But as soon as you get to the next level, the game gets even harder, and if you don't want the fun to stop, you keep buying lives and points to continue playing. Some players get hooked to the game and keep buying the consumable in-app purchases for more points.

If your product isn't a natural fit to the subscription or the consumable models, there are plenty of other strong monetization strategies. The next strategy to consider is a slight reversal in how we have been thinking about monetization. While the subscription and consumables strategies depend on long-term customer relationship over which you make money, wouldn't it be great if you could just charge a significant amount of money upfront? That is available if you position your business as a high-end brand.

If your business is not a high-end brand, you can make a larger catalog of products available for a lower price per product. Sometimes one person can snap up a bunch of products on a sale that together add to significant revenue equating to one high-end sale or a year's worth of purchases in a subscription model. I like to use this model because it leaves customers happy that they get great value and I am happy about generating more revenue.

3. How to turn clients for any business into long-term clients

You may be planning to use social media to attract new customers as a part of your marketing strategy, but social media is equally if not more effective for retaining existing customers?

If you get your customers to subscribe to your email updates or follow you on Twitter, Facebook, LinkedIn, YouTube, podcast, or sign up for your updates in any other way, you can promote new products, services, or discounts to your social media followers indefinitely - possibly for years. Plus, the more social media platforms someone follows you on, the more likely they are to see your promotions. The more promotions they see, the more likely they are to engage with that promotion. Social media updates also help to re-engage people who may have wanted to buy from you but didn't follow through, or past customers who could use what you are selling, but need an extra little reminder and enticement like possibly a sale announcement. Of course, be careful not to over-promote. If they see promotions too often, they might get irritated, unfollow you, and you will lose the ability to promote to them entirely.

If you are able to engage your social media followers, your marketing can be just as effective as a subscription or the consumables model since people will be buying from you on a regular basis.

You might wonder which social network is most effective in getting people to re-engage with your business. The answer is that multiple points of contact is better, but if you had to pick one, it is email. Most online marketers place a great deal of importance on email. If you create, grow, and maintain a highly engaged email list, it can be a powerful tool for you to generate many sales from your customers for months and years to come.

Social networks tend to change in popularity. The most popular one used to be MySpace. Then it was Twitter. Then Facebook, Instagram, and tomorrow it will be something else. But email has remained popular and effective since the Internet began.

PART 2: EXECUTION

Planning is great. But without execution, nothing comes to fruition. This book wouldn't do right by you if it covered just how to plan. There must also be a transition to implementing the plan.

In the second part of the book, we'll explore the wisdom of the greatest books on entrepreneurship to see how much value they put on planning vs. implementation. After that, you will learn how to make yourself effective at executing everything your business requires.

Chapter 11:
Classic Entrepreneurship Books And Their Takeaways

"All books are divisible into two classes, the books of the hour, and the books of all time."

- John Ruskin

This chapter will introduce you to some of the most revolutionary books on entrepreneurship of all time and highlight the most important business principles they teach. These are core fundamentals that have withstood the test of time. By the end of this chapter, you should have a clearer understanding of precisely what you should focus on in your entrepreneurship journey.

Before we start, here is a brief summary of these core entrepreneurship principles. As you read this chapter, notice how often the best books from the past 100 years will echo these ideas:

- Persistence and hard work - not talent or money - are the main ingredients for success.

- Planning is useful, but over-planning can be a form of procrastination and therefore harmful. Action and progress are needed relatively early.

- Too much planning can cause you to never start.

- Start small and build up to your bigger vision over time.

- Practice self-awareness and self-exploration so you can choose correct life goals and business goals that will help you achieve your life goals.

- Have intense focus, passion, and drive toward your goals.

- Surround yourself with people who will uplift, inspire, and help you reach your goals.

- The business you pursue should be aligned with your passions and life goals so it can give you long-term fulfillment.

- In addition to hard work, focus on your productivity and efficiency so you can get more done each day.

Disclaimer: These summaries are not intended to replace reading of the actual books. Reading the books will give you value beyond these summaries.

1. Think and Grow Rich by Napoleon Hill

Published in 1937, this is one of the oldest business books, and perhaps the one still most referenced. It has withstood the test of time and is recommended reading for first-time entrepreneurs.

There is a famous quote in philosophy by Alfred Whitehead that "the safest general characterization of the European philosophical tradition is that it consists of a series of footnotes to Plato," which suggests that Plato who lived over 2,000 years ago, planted the seed and started the conversations that were merely followed up on by other philosophers.

Just as European philosophy's last 2,000 years are a footnote to Plato, it often feels that the last (almost) 100 years of business books have been a footnote to Napoleon Hill's *Think and Grow Rich*.

In this book, Napoleon Hill interviewed the most successful entrepreneurs of his generation in a quest to learn the true secrets that lead to their massive wealth and success, and summed it up in 13 core principles.

Principle 1: Make sure you *want* wealth bad enough

Principle 2: *Believe* that you can achieve success

Principle 3: Use of affirmations (auto suggestion) to help you believe you can achieve your goals and give you *confidence*

Principle 4: *Gain specialized knowledge* and continue learning and improving

Principle 5: Boost your imagination and ability to come up with *new ways to solve problems*

Principle 6: Balance organized planning with *taking action*

Principle 7: Be *decisive*

Principle 8: Be *persistent* - don't stop until you get what you want

Principle 9: Surround yourself with helpful people or join *mastermind groups*

Principle 10: Choose a *compatible life partner*

Principle 11: Master *positivity* and get rid of negative emotions

Principle 12: *Associate with smart people* and learn from them

Principle 13: Gain a "sixth sense" which is another way to say that *with experience*, you will have accurate gut reactions, and you'll develop a sense for making correct business decisions

Principle one, wanting wealth bad enough, is an important one. Many people start a business because it seems cool or fun. But it is difficult to start one and see it through to success. Only do it if you truly must. And if you do, work on soft skills like keeping up your confidence and being positive. There is also a big emphasis on surrounding yourself with good people in your professional and personal life. All these things will help to carry you forward through difficult times.

There is also point relevant to the subject of this book, which is to make sure you plan well yet not to spend too much time planning because over-planning can often result in never starting, which can be worse than trying and failing. If you are a planner by nature, note principle seven, which is decisiveness. Begin practicing it. Unless you have a good reason to do so, don't put off making decisions. Give yourself enough time to think through potential pros and cons of a decision, and decide. You won't always be correct, but overall it will be better than postponing your decisions.

So, plan, start, and be persistent over time. Conviction and passion will give you the drive to persist. Long-term hard work combined with a good social foundation that gives you support and confidence will help you succeed.

2. *The E-Myth Revisited* by Michael E. Gerber

This book was originally written in 1990 and re-written in 2004. It explains why most businesses fail. E-Myth stands for Entrepreneurial Myth, and no, it isn't some kind of a new iPhone (ePhone).

Many people think that because they know how to perform the technical aspect of a business, they can run the entire business. But the business needs many additional skills like marketing, management, leadership, and building systems and processes so the business runs smoothly. This book identifies three key roles that the business owner must grow into.

1) Technician for hands-on technical work

2) Manager for organization

3) Entrepreneur for vision and growth

Many people start as a technician. They can do the job. For example, they can fix a roof, write software, or provide any other kind of service. That is fine in the beginning, but as the business grows, the technician must evolve and learn managerial and leadership skills.

Most readers of this book are technicians who have a skill and want to turn it into a business. Michael Gerber trains the technician on how to become a manager and gain the necessary leadership and management skills. After that, you learn how to grow your business to scale, including how to make the business largely systematized and replicable for other locations or franchises. The focus isn't to build a franchise, but rather to make replicable systems to help the business scale, and for the technician to be able to step back.

The book also discusses structuring life goals, business goals, and the day-to-day organizational strategy of your business, and making them align.

This book's first major takeaway: Organization, systems, and procedures are needed to take your business past the technician phase. You must acquire new skills beyond technical ones and understand the big-picture requirements.

This book's second major takeaway: Plan for the business and lifestyle you want so you can be in it passionately long-term. If your passion is not there, you will want to do something else due to lack of fulfillment.

3. The Four Steps to the Epiphany by Steve Blank

Steve Blank is a Stanford Business School professor who has previously built three billion-dollar companies using one core principle: The Customer Development methodology.

The idea behind this principle is that gaining consumer feedback and anecdotal experiences is key to developing a successful business. *Before* building a product or providing a particular service, you must seek out potential customers and ask them various questions, such as whether they would use/buy the service and if they currently have any of the assumed pain points. This market feedback is invaluable and prevents you from basing your work on false, theoretical assumptions. Customer insights will help you build a product or service they love and will be more likely to buy. Feedback can also give you insight to why potential customers might not buy your product, which would save you a lot of time and money by preventing you from creating it.

The book's rallying cry is to: "get out of the building." It is a call to get out of your office or garage where you are dreaming about and possibly overthinking your idea, and seek out your potential customers for feedback. Talk to them to understand their attitude toward your idea.

Many people worry about having their idea stolen after talking about it with anyone who is not already a part of the business. That is a common concern among first-time entrepreneurs. It is almost always an overblown fear. Nevertheless, there are a few ways to decrease the risk of having your idea stolen. The first is to only work with ethical people you can trust. Another is to ask people to sign an NDA (Non-Disclosure Agreement). And another is to be selective of what you share in different situations, because most of the time you can discuss a general idea without giving away your "secret sauce."

4. The Lean Startup by Eric Ries

Eric Ries is a student of Steve Blank's. His theories were built as perfect complements to Steve Blank's Customer Development process. In his book, Eric Ries outlines two important concepts: the MVP (Minimum Viable Product) and the Lean Startup process.

To illustrate how Steve Blank's and Eric Ries's methodologies work together, let's assume you've gone through the Customer Development process and you are ready to execute your plan. Do you build your grandiose vision right away? According to Eric Ries, the answer is no. Instead, you build an MVP - the *minimum viable* version of your *product.*

Once you build your MVP, you must immediately let customers use it so you can gather feedback about the live product. In the beginning this can be your beta launch stage, but it is good to continue doing this far beyond the beta stage, releasing your product to more people each time you make improvements. Ask the people using every new version of the product what is good and bad about it. After you gather each round of assessments, go back to product development and make a few small improvements based on that feedback. After those improvements are made, release the new version of the product and repeat the process again. This is the key to the Lean Startup process - small iterations of the product in order to improve rapidly.

This type of rapid prototyping will help you improve your product quickly and with little wasted effort. You won't waste resources building wrong features that people don't even want because you are making improvements based on customer feedback and not guesses. As your product matures, you don't have to get feedback at such rapid intervals, but never stop it entirely.

This fits well with Napoleon Hill's outlook on business planning. The Customer Development process is something you do during planning and Eric Ries's methodology helps you launch faster and improve quickly rather than over-planning while sitting on the sidelines.

5. *Purple Cow* by Seth Godin

Cows are common farm animals. Once you've seen one or a few, you might not get too excited when you see your tenth cow. They are mostly the same. But what if you saw a cow that was all purple? Purple cows don't exist in nature so you'd get surprised, stop, and take a closer look at it. Business and products can also feel mostly the same to customers. Seth Godin's idea is that a business must stand out among its competitors by being different; it must be a purple cow among a field of regular cows. When you are creative, bold, or unique, you stand out and get noticed.

It can take courage to stand out. It isn't always easy to do. It takes imagination and isn't without occasional embarrassments and naysayers. But it can be exactly the advantage you need to get attention and more clients. You can apply the Purple Cow concept to your business overall, and every headline you write, every article you post, every product you plan, and everything you do.

A simple example can illustrate the effectiveness of this concept. Early in my career as an entrepreneur, when I started my group hiking business, I wasn't doing anything unique, and those regular hikes were not getting much attention. But as soon as I posted a hike called "Low Tide Hunt For Long-Lost Shipwrecks Along San Francisco Coast" a number of local news sites picked up my event and even the Sunday paper published a story about it without my knowing.

Eye-catching hike themes were my purple cows. They helped my hikes get attention and attendance began to exceed maximum capacity, and turned a failure into a success.

If I had to spend money running ads to get the same amount of traffic as those eye-catching headlines generated, it would have cost me thousands of dollars, but I got that traffic for free by doing something unique.

Just don't get discouraged if at first you don't succeed. Most people who succeed are persistent. If I had lost confidence and quit organizing the hikes at an early stage, I would have never gotten the idea for my purple cow and the success would have never come. Even some of my later purple cow attempts like a "Spring Blooming Flower Hike" failed and got no attendance. Just power through the small failures and keep working on being the most unique and interesting business among your competitors. The difference between success and failure can simply be not quitting early.

6. *Outliers* by Malcolm Gladwell

Outliers examines why some people fail and some succeed, which is a popular topic in entrepreneurship conversations. Most people remember this book for its unscientific but catchy and plausible "ten-thousand-hour rule," which is roughly the amount of practice it takes to become great at something. Gladwell attests that in order to become one of the best in your field, you must deliberately practice your craft to improve your skills for ten thousand hours.

Another takeaway from this book is that innate abilities are overrated. What differentiates us is our ability to try - not stand on the sidelines, but actually getting started. This echoes Napoleon Hill, doesn't it?

Another interesting anecdote from the book is that your birth month matters. Imagine students in any grade year. Some students are eleven months older than others. At six or seven years old, that makes a tremendous difference in physical and mental abilities. Older kids in the same grade year are often perceived as better at many things and are given more opportunities to excel. This gives them the confidence to keep pursuing that field and allows them to develop those skills further and make use of them throughout life. Conversely, according to Gladwell, younger students tend to have lower confidence, which leads to lower persistence, lower skill development, and on average less success in life.

The older kids accidentally fall into more confidence which often carries over to persistence and eventual success. Confidence is another major principle from Napoleon Hill.

7. The 4-Hour Work Week by Tim Ferriss

This is a relatively controversial book with mixed results for entrepreneurs who pursue its strategies, but it is quite popular. Tim Ferris has established himself as one of the premiere business authors, and this book catapulted him to the top of the genre.

Early in his book, Tim Ferris introduces the concept of relative income. It illustrates that with today's technology, a person can automate their business and thus only work a few hours a week from anywhere in the world where cost of living might be cheap. Tim Ferris contrasts that with the traditional office job, where a person might earn a larger annual salary, but spend more hours working and commuting while also incurring a higher cost of living.

The book makes a point that to be rich is to have a lot of money, but to be truly wealthy is to have a lot of extra time and do what you want with your life.

While this is a great concept, its implications are disputed. It is easy to imagine how this created an army of people who don't want to work, and want to travel the world and magically make money online instead. This has caused many "facepalm moments" in my business coaching practice where I've had to explain that no, it isn't truly *that* easy. You still have to work hard. Even if you are working ten hours a week from a remote island, there will always be someone on a remote island next to yours, working eighty hours per week, using the same strategies you are using, and outcompeting you. This book underestimates hard work and passionate pursuit of goals. Think back to Napoleon Hill's very first rule to success which states that you must have passionate desire for your goals, without which it is difficult to have the long-term motivation and do persistent hard work.

What I like about Tim's book is his point that it is important to eliminate time consuming and wasteful tasks that don't get you closer to your goals. Tim Ferris gives examples of TV, news, and other media nonsense, which often add negativity to your life, don't contribute much beyond senseless entertainment, and take up a lot of your time - time that is not put toward achieving your goals.

The next idea in the book is about outsourcing tasks to online freelancers so you can save time. When *The 4-Hour Work Week* was published, this was relatively groundbreaking, and only a few years later everyone became aware of outsourcing. But there is one major pitfall many entrepreneurs fall into with that. Outsourcing tasks does not mean outsourcing most of the work in your business or handing things to a freelancer and hoping for the best. If you don't have a good grasp of your business strategies and tasks you are outsourcing, your freelancers will either be ineffective from poor directions or simply see this as an opportunity to take advantage of you by telling you whatever you want to hear as long as you keep paying.

You will only be able to make good business decisions, delegate the right tasks, and correctly instruct freelancers after you've worked hard and gained enough experience. There is no way to skip this.

A good rule of thumb about outsourcing is that paying hourly low wages does not mean cheap. A low-cost and low-skill worker may take much longer to do a task than a higher skilled worker. Not only would that negate all the supposed savings, but a highly-skilled worker with more experience can also make more independent decisions, think on their feet, and deliver better results while requiring less of your time managing them. It is often better to pay more for quality work than cheaper wages that get you shoddy results and work you might have to re-do.

In summary, while this book can be quite helpful if its strategies are interpreted correctly, its effect has often been the contrary. It isn't Tim's fault, but rather the law of unintended consequences. The book has an exciting premise but fails when it deviates from time-proven concepts.

8. How to Win Friends and Influence People by Dale Carnegie

This is another great book that has withstood the test of time. I personally love this book because it began to explore what resembles Emotional

Intelligence before Emotional Intelligence was established as a distinct field. Here's a summary of Dale Carnegie's key lessons.

Lesson 1: You can't win an argument.

Ironically, not only does arguing have a high chance of creating animosity, but mostly ends with both parties feeling even more convinced that they are absolutely right. Even if you win an argument, you might still lose in a bigger sense because the other person may be hurt, lose confidence, dislike you, or simply no longer want to interact with you (unfriending or ghosting you in today's vernacular).

If you feel that you are about to get into an argument with someone, take a step back and give yourself a few seconds to reflect on whether it is worth the time, energy, and possible negative outcomes. Those few seconds might be just the amount of time you need to resolve the situation in a more constructive manner.

Lesson 2: Never tell a person they are wrong.

If you tell someone they are wrong, they may take offense because they believe they are correct. Instead of directly stating that someone is wrong, ask them why they believe what they believe and talk through the situation with them. If they are indeed wrong, it will become clear to them as you explore the situation in the conversation. That is more constructive and you have a higher chance of convincing them.

The takeaway is that you have to make people understand the situation so they can come to conclusions on their own rather than imposing your opinion on them.

Lesson 3: Ask respectfully and in question form instead of giving orders if you need something done.

You can rephrase statements into question forms. For example, you can say "can you please help me with this task?" instead of "do this task." No one likes being told what to do and people immediately feel negativity and anger at the person commanding them. But when people are asked politely, they are naturally more willing to comply. The task itself is often an afterthought and they gladly do it.

Lesson 4: Remember names.

This might feel obvious, but remembering a person's name has obvious benefits. People feel better when you address them by their name. It is a sign that you respect and value them. This little bit of personal attention can go a long way.

If you don't remember a person's name, it might cause you to have slight panic and act awkwardly around them, and possibly even unnecessarily avoiding them.

To improve this basic skill, try using the person's name briefly after they are introduced or ask for a business card if appropriate. Also be sure to end the conversation by using their name to create a mental association. Another tip for remembering names is to write down the person's name and even a descriptive sentence in a memo on their phone or in a notebook right after you meet them. Some people use memory tricks in which they associate a person's name with something that happened so that the association would help them recall the person's name. For example, if you meet someone named Mark in a mall, quickly make a mental note to yourself that this person is "mall Mark." You'll never tell them that, but you will be more likely to remember their name.

Lesson 5: Talk in terms of other people's interests.

Ask people about their interests and what they like. Taking the time to listen to them will help them enjoy the conversation, and since they are having that conversation with you, they will feel like they enjoy spending time with you and will like you more. It is that simple. One of the core takeaways from the book is to take *genuine* interest in people. Here is a quote from the book that resonates:

"You can make more friends in two months by becoming interested in other people than you can in two years by trying to get other people interested in you."

9. See You At The Top: 25th Anniversary Edition by Zig Ziglar

If you've never seen Zig Ziglar speak, it is a real treat. He is an amazing public speaker. YouTube some of his videos. They are motivational and entertaining.

This book feels like an echo of Napoleon Hill's book. Zig Ziglar has six principles of success:

1) Manage your self-image and build confidence

2) Foster relationships with others

3) Set great goals

4) Adjust your attitude and mindset

5) Work hard and be persistent

6) Possess a deep desire to succeed

Zig Ziglar emphasizes cultivating a positive self-image and gives a sixteen-step guide on making people more confident, which includes things like positive self-talk (affirmations) and blocking out negativity.

When it comes to cultivating relationships, just like Napoleon Hill did before him, Zig Ziglar recommends to associate with other successful people. He also recommends having healthy personal relationships like a fulfilling marriage.

Zig Ziglar also discusses goal setting and the paths to reach those goals. He recommends writing your goals down and documenting your progress over time. Zig Ziglar recommends to set big, challenging, but attainable goals to keep you motivated and excited about the big challenge and big rewards.

Since your goals will be big, Zig Ziglar recommends that you break them down into many easily achievable steps and give yourself a long-term deadline such as a year or longer to reach the big goal. But keep doing the small daily tasks to keep getting closer to your goals.

Zig Ziglar also goes on to make a distinction between your self-image and your attitude. While your self-image is how you see yourself, your attitude is how you feel toward the rest of the world. Are you a positive person or do you let minor hiccups distract you and steer you off course? If you feel like you might not be good enough or the world is somehow aligned against you, find a way to defeat such mindset and gain confidence. Ultimately, everything will be up to your execution and not external forces.

When it comes to work, Zig Ziglar urges people to stop expecting handouts or a free lunch, and instead focus intensely on doing the work to reach your goals. He bases much of his own logic on a famous Chuck Swindoll quote: "Life is ten percent of what happens to you, and ninety percent of how you react to it."

Zig Ziglar also makes the point we've seen in other great business books that you must not only desire great outcomes, but do the work to get there. Many people incessantly talk about wanting to succeed, but don't do the work. Hard work is what will get you to the top.

10. The Miracle Morning by Hal Elrod

This isn't necessarily a business book. It is a book on how to become more self-aware and productive so that you can make ideal life goal decisions. After all, your business is only one tool to help you achieve your life goals.

According to Hal Elrod, the key to success lies in how you approach your morning. In fact, it starts with the evening before that morning. Every evening, make a plan for the next day and what you want to accomplish. This will help you wake up with motivation and drive to go after what you want.

For people who like to sleep in, he recommends setting an alarm and putting your alarm clock beyond arm's reach so you would need to get up to turn it off. Once you get up, go brush your teeth and take a shower, and you will be alert and ready to tackle the day's challenges.

Once you've woken up, you are ready for what Hal Elrod refers to as Life S.A.V.E.R.S. which is an acronym.

S stands for silence. Begin every day with silence. It will reduce stress and anxiety, and help you gain self-awareness.

A stands for affirmations. We've seen this old friend before.

V stands for visualizations. Visualize what you want and do the work for achieving what you want.

E stands for exercise. Do at least some light exercise every morning to get energy and boost mental health.

R stands for reading. Reading as a key to success. (Kind of an obvious point. Perhaps Hal Elrod just needed to make the catchy acronym work.)

S stands for scribbling. By this, Hal Elrod means to write down big and little goals, and write a to-do list to stay organized throughout the day.

These "life savers" might not seem like much, but small lifestyle changes can significantly impact your focus and performance.

To hit the ground running every morning, at the end of each workday, create a to-do list for the next day. It gives your mind a chance to process it, "sleep on it," and get comfortable approaching those tasks, which might even get you excited about them. Writing the list can even ease stress. Seeing the items on a page can make them seem less daunting. Plus, you won't have to worry about forgetting anything since it is all written down.

Experience this for yourself. For the next few evenings, create a to-do list for your next day. It can make a big difference in your productivity. And if you can get some light exercise in before you start working, it will do wonders for your positivity and enthusiasm throughout your workday.

11. Additional Books Related To Planning

There are a few additional books specifically related to planning that deserve honorable mentions.

1) *The 1-Page Marketing Plan* by Allan Dib outlines marketing tactics for the period before, during, and after you launch your marketing campaign.

Before you commence work on any business, you must have a great plan for promoting it so a marketing plan is a necessary complement to a business plan. If you recall, one of the biggest business planning mistakes is not having a marketing plan.

2) Another book related to planning is the *Business Model Generation* by Alexander Osterwalder. It helps you create a complete business model by first focusing on separate parts of your business, and then making them work perfectly with one another. It is helpful if you want to dive deeper into your business model and ensure that everything is planned well before starting a business.

3) I should also mention that I wrote a companion book to the book you are reading, called the *Marketing Plan Template & Example*. It takes a similar approach as this book by starting you with only a three sentence marketing plan, and letting you work up in complexity from there. The beauty of this book is that by the end of it, you should end up with a marketing plan that is effective for your unique situation.

12. Honorable Mentions

1) *Emotional Intelligence* by Daniel Goleman

Emotional Intelligence is a highly learnable skill that every professional must attain. It is a combination of sharpened self-awareness, social awareness, and being able to identify the mood of those around you. It helps you understand and manage your own emotions, emotions of others, and use them productively instead of destructively. Imagine an athlete who gets frustrated or angry. In the moment, they can either do something damaging to themselves, their team, or another player, or they can channel their anger to play harder and win. Being able to manage your emotions is at the root of making such productive decisions many times each day.

2) *Elon Musk: Tesla, SpaceX, and the Quest for a Fantastic Future* by Elon Musk

This is a biographical book, but it is about one of the most fascinating entrepreneurs today. Elon Musk has succeeded in building three revolutionary businesses *at the same time*. He is a big-picture thinker and an intelligent guy.

It is an inspiring book for entrepreneurs with big dreams with many lessons for aspiring entrepreneurs. Just keep in mind that for most entrepreneurs, the rule of thumb is to pick one business and focus on it intensely - not three businesses like Elon.

3) *Steve Jobs* by Walter Isaacson

This is a biography about Steve Jobs based on interviews of Jobs himself and his family. It gives a glimpse into the mind of a brilliant innovator.

4) *20 Principles of Productivity* by Alex Genadinik

Apologies for recommending my own book here. I've been searching for a comprehensive productivity book for a long time, but even though I recommended Hal Elrod's productivity book earlier in this chapter, I have not found a comprehensive productivity book so I decided to write my own. The aim of this book is to turn you into an absolute productivity machine by covering all facets of personal productivity from many angles. By the end of this book, you should have the knowledge for how to produce more and better work from now on, and every day for the rest of your career.

Next chapter's 50 success skills is a glimpse into the comprehensive approach of this productivity book.

13. Summary

There are many more wonderful books that can be included in this list. If your favorite book isn't mentioned, I apologize. The books in the list illustrate the main themes of entrepreneurship which are to have passion, plan but not over-plan, surround yourself with great people, work hard, stay confident in the face of setbacks, and be persistent.

Chapter 12:
50 Success Skills

"The way to get started is to quit talking and begin doing"

-Walt Disney

As echoed in classic entrepreneurship books, hard and consistent work is one of the top ingredients to success. This is also a theme in my coaching practice. While planning is important, the entrepreneur has to work passionately and intensely for a long time, producing high-quality work - not just quantity. There is no replacement for hard work, persistence, and competence.

I've assembled a list of 50 success skills for entrepreneurs that help you work more efficiently and produce higher-quality work. Many of these skills can be learned. They will help you become a much more effective entrepreneur, and can be used throughout your career. I call them "Success Skills" because almost every one of them will help you produce more work, higher quality work, and the right kind of work with less wasted effort, all of which will lead to better results and ultimately success.

This chapter is a crash course on the 50 skills. It is not meant to make you immediately brilliant at each right away. Most of these skills are big topics that have entire books devoted to them. They can only be covered briefly in this book, but if any of these skills interest you, that may shape your further learning. If you ever begin to doubt yourself or your abilities, refer to this list of 50 skills for ideas of what may be missing in your approach.

1. List of the 50 success skills

Browse through each skill, and reflect on them individually for a few seconds so they don't blend into one another. After that, we'll dive deeper into when each of these comes into play.

SKILLS FOR BEFORE BEGINNING YOUR WORK

1) Self-awareness and self-exploration to choose the right life goals for yourself

2) Figuring out and deciding on your life purpose and direction

3) Goal setting to set large, achievable goals that will excite and motivate you

4) Intense drive or excitement about achieving your goals

5) Planning how you will achieve your goals and outlining a strategy (not to be confused with business planning)

6) Focusing your projects by narrowing down the projects you work on via eliminating projects that don't bring you closer to your goals (not to be confused with ability to focus on an immediate task like reading, writing, or paying attention)

SKILLS NEEDED TO DO DAILY WORK

7) Self-discipline

8) Extrinsic and intrinsic motivation

9) Building "healthy" productive habits that make work natural

10) Identifying procrastination triggers and reversing procrastination

11) Boosting your ability to focus on a single immediate task

12) Eliminating interruptions

13) Organizing your work environment to be more productive

14) Time management and realistic scheduling

15) Consistent daily work

SKILLS TO BOOST INTELLIGENCE AND BRAIN FUNCTION

16) Boosting IQ (Intelligence Quotient) - small improvements possible

17) Boosting EQ (Emotional Intelligence) - large improvements possible

18) Boosting creativity

19) Learning problem solving

20) Logical reasoning, thinking ahead, planning strategically, being aware of logical fallacies

21) Boosting memory (memory is underrated in how much it boosts intelligence)

KNOWING HOW AND WHEN TO GET HELP

22) Getting coaching

23) Joining mastermind groups

24) Partaking in peer networking and learning

25) Taking advantage of tools like apps, planners, and calendars to improve efficiency

MAINTAINING YOUR HEALTH FOR PHYSICAL AND MENTAL ABILITIES

26) Getting enough sleep and rest

27) Maintaining a proper diet, preferably one that boosts brain function and gives you energy

28) Exercising regularly for peak mental health and alertness

29) Fostering a supportive relationship environment

MANAGEMENT AND LEADERSHIP SKILLS

30) Leadership of yourself first and foremost

31) Leadership of others and building leaders within your organization

32) Finding the right business partners and co-founders

33) Outsourcing

34) Hiring

35) Team building

36) Meeting productivity and collaboration

37) Team productivity and project management

38) Process automation, building business systems, and optimizing your business systems to function most efficiently and be replicable

39) Decision making and prioritization

40) Conflict management and resolution

PSYCHOLOGY / PHILOSOPHY / MINDSET

41) Dealing with pressure

42) Stress management

43) Building confidence and self-esteem, starting with affirmations (sometimes using overconfidence as a tool)

44) Questioning existing methods and finding better ones

FASTER LEARNING AND SKILL ACQUISITION

45) Retention skills

46) Speed reading

47) Note taking

48) Brainstorming skills

49) Application and practice of skills

50) Focus on continuing education

The Japanese term "Kaizen" is the notion that a person is constantly and continuously improving. The same applies to business. Most of the skills in the 50 success skills list help during the execution phase of the business. My goal with this list is to help you execute at a higher level which will have direct benefits for your business.

2. The REAL challenge for your business

There is a pattern in almost every industry. A disproportionate amount of revenue goes to the top companies and almost all other companies struggle.

For example, in the taxi app space, the major winner is Uber. The second company is Lyft. The third company is behind by such a wide margin that most people would struggle to name it or recognize its name if it was stated. In social networks, there are Facebook, Instagram, Pinterest, Twitter, a few others, and a steep drop after that. In book sales, the difference between the #1 bestselling book in the world and the #100 is also very wide. The salary gap between a top athlete and the one ranked #100 in almost any sport is also tremendous. As the classic ABBA song goes, "the winner takes it all."

While starting a business is a great first step, to become truly successful or wealthy, you can't just be pretty good or even good. You must be great, dominate your industry, and defeat all or almost all competition. So how do you dominate a lucrative or a competitive industry?

I have good news and bad news. The good news is that the path to win is known and within reach for most. The bad news is that if you want to be the best, you must compete against some of the most brilliant people and companies in the world and come out on top. It is easy to be the best soccer player at your local park, but if you want to attain true success, you must become the Lionel Messi of your era, and that is difficult.

If you don't follow soccer, Lionel Messi is arguably the best soccer player of all time, and he accomplished this while being born with physical disadvantages and had to take growth hormones just to reach a height of five feet and five inches, which is shorter than most adults, let alone world class athletes.

The rule is: Wildly competent execution - no excuses.

3. Path to business success

The path to success may not be linear, but typically follows these three steps:

Step 1: Identify your true passion and choose goals on which you will focus intensely

Step 2: Plan how you will get there

Step 3: Execute consistently and relentlessly without stopping until you achieve your goals

Try not to get bogged down in steps one and two because the hardest part is step three, the execution. Nearly all of the 50 success skills are aimed to make you and your employees as brilliant as possible on a second-to-second and day-to-day basis in every aspect of execution, ranging from how you handle your emotions to your ability to focus to your leadership of yourself and of others.

But before focusing on execution, let's make sure you are working on the right life project.

4. Our life projects

Choosing the right life path is arguably our most important decision. The choice itself is a lifelong process because you are a different person in your teens than you are in your twenties, thirties, fifties, and older. Your brain changes. How you see the world changes and, frankly, the world around you changes over the course of a few decades.

To ensure that you choose and stay on the right life path for you, it is recommended that entrepreneurs practice self-awareness, introspection, and mindfulness while surrounding themselves with people who can be sounding boards and brainstorming partners. Self-awareness and advice from credible people are the best tools we have to ensure that we make correct choices regarding our life trajectory. It isn't always easy to practice self-awareness, but everyone owes it to themselves. As Plato put it, "An unexamined life is not worth living."

It is OK to make mistakes, and it is better to change life direction late rather than never starting anything at all in fear of making mistakes.

Once you've decided on your life trajectory, it will be easier to choose goals that will excite you, and you will be able to create a plan to achieve those goals (not to be confused with a business plan). Motivation and drive will come from choosing the right goals.

Once you have your plan to reach your goals, you are ready to begin the work. It can be scary and exciting. Here is a small excerpt from one of my favorite poems that helped to reassure me whenever I felt self-doubt throughout my entrepreneurship journey and should make you proud of the courage that it took you to become an entrepreneur.

"Two roads diverged in a wood, and I—

I took the one less traveled by,

And that has made all the difference."

- Robert Frost

5. Eliminating waste in your schedule

Proper time management will immediately help you execute better by freeing up more of your time to work on the most important things, and keeping a calendar is one of the first steps in time management. Keeping a calendar is a great way to stay on track, monitor progress, and organize your tasks. It will also help you figure out if you're spending your time on things that may be detracting from more vital tasks.

If you already keep a calendar, go through the things you did in the past four weeks and note how many tasks you had that didn't get you closer to your goals. If you don't already keep a calendar, start one now to see how much waste there is in your schedule. Seeing it will help you identify wastes of time and remove them, giving you more time to work on what's important.

Determining whether your business brings you closer to your goals is a part of this exercise. There may be other activities that are more effective at getting you to your goals. Check your calendar to make sure that you don't have something more important to do than your business. After having done this exercise, if you still feel that your business is the right tool to get you closer to your goals, it is a good reason to continue pursuing your business. If not, the business might actually be the distraction you can consider eliminating so you can free up time to work on things that do bring you closer to your goals.

Examples of something more important than your business might be making your music if you are a musician, studying if you are a student, or parenting if you are a parent. You can still pursue a business if you are a musician, student, or a parent. The distinction is that you first choose what's *most important* for you, and if it is something that isn't your business, make sure that you devote enough time to the truly important tasks.

6. Business planning

As we've seen in Napoleon Hill's research, there is a delicate balance between too little and too much business planning. If you don't plan enough or correctly, the business has a small chance of surviving. If you over-plan, you run the risk of never starting. It's important to toe the line, feel confident in your planning, and start the execution phase without over-evaluating.

You may wonder what the ideal timetable for planning is, but every business and life situation is different. While it is impossible to give a foolproof timetable, a good rule of thumb is that if you are planning for over two weeks, start devoting at least 20% of the work you are putting toward planning into doing something. That doesn't have to be fully starting the business, but it might be starting your fundraising effort or starting to look for website designers or practicing some business skill that will be necessary once you start. Don't invest much money at this stage, but begin doing *work*. And if you are able to afford it, your budget doesn't have to be zero. After all, you are working on your dreams.

7. Don't trust yourself - test yourself

In all my years of working with entrepreneurs, I've never heard anyone explicitly say "I'll completely flake on myself" or "I won't work hard" or "I'll get frustrated and quit almost immediately," but unfortunately that is what happens to most people starting a business. It's easy to hype yourself up when you are excited about a concept, but the true test comes when you have to push yourself the extra mile to keep putting the work into your idea.

Life happens . . . or people happen to themselves. It is OK. We all get excited, work ourselves up, and calm down. Don't trust yourself when you are excited. Test yourself in action.

That test is you beginning to do the work to make your business happen. Set a day on your calendar to begin doing the work. If that day goes by, and a week goes by, and another week goes by, and not much daily work has been done, that is a signal to look into productivity fundamentals from the 50 success skills, specifically things like discipline, reversing procrastination, building healthy work habits, organizing your workspace, eliminating interruptions, managing your time, and finding the right motivation. These are precisely the skills to get you to begin doing the work and keep you working daily.

8. Once you are consistently doing work

Starting will get you ahead of more than 50% of the people out there who talk about their dreams but never start. Consistently working will get you ahead of 60%, 70%, then 80%, and perhaps even 90% of your competition as you become better at what you do. Those numbers are deceiving. They might seem good, but it is not enough. Recall that most industries are lopsided and only the leaders win big. To be truly successful, you need to be the best and get to the top 1% or 2%. To get there, you'll have to outcompete some of the most competent people and businesses. It isn't easy so keep improving the quality of your work by becoming better at the remaining skills on the list of 50 success skills, and before you know it, you'll find yourself dominating your industry.

Chapter 13:
Making You A Better Entrepreneur & Starting Your Business

"Ideas are easy. Implementation is hard."

-Guy Kawasaki

This chapter is a crash course on additional skills, mindset, and knowledge needed to start and run a successful business. Each of the topics covered is broad and could have its own separate book. These will be brief introductions to guide you on what you might want to research next.

1. Procrastination

People procrastinate for different reasons. For most people, procrastination is a habit. A habit is a learned behavior that can be stopped if you form a new healthier habit to replace the old habit.

Studies show that it takes about three weeks of daily behavior to form a new habit. You must force yourself to do things in a new way, and after a few weeks you will no longer need to force yourself. You will just do the new, healthier behavior naturally without thinking about it.

The hardest part of breaking your procrastination habit is taking the first steps to reverse your previously learned behavior, replacing it with another, and not relapsing later.

2. Motivation

There are two kinds of motivation: Intrinsic and extrinsic.

Intrinsic motivation comes from inside you. It is an inner drive you feel when you are excited about something and doing what you love. This is usually a long-term motivation toward something. It is that strong inner drive that the great entrepreneurship authors wrote about.

Extrinsic motivation is typically short-term motivation you might get from something external like an energetic song, motivational pep talk, or a reward for yourself like a fun trip or a snack, the motivational effects of which dissipate within minutes, hours, or days.

While both types of motivation are useful, intrinsic motivation is much more helpful to encourage you over the lifetime of your business. If you are working on well-chosen goals and have put your life trajectory on a path that is right for you, much of your motivation will naturally be intrinsic. On the other hand, if you've mistakenly chosen the wrong goals, given into external pressures, and are not working on the things that excite you, you will be naturally less motivated, which will lead to lower interest in your work and lower quality execution, followed by low confidence. Lack of motivation, inadequate execution, or low confidence can be a signals that you chose a goal that isn't ideal.

It all starts with getting to know yourself better and becoming more self aware so you understand what's right for YOU to pursue. Intrinsic motivation will follow.

3. Focus, Pomodoro technique, eliminating interruptions

Once you conquer your procrastination challenges, find the right motivation, and begin working, the next major issue to conquer is how to get more accomplished and doing your best quality work while you work.

There are many tactics and strategies to boost your productivity, but arguably the single most effective way to dramatically improve your productivity is to improve the quality of your focus. The more singular, intense, and prolonged your focus is on a given task, the better and faster that task will go.

Your phone, social media, extra open tabs on your browser, multitasking, and people nearby who might distract you, all decrease your productivity by interrupting your focus. The more you can reduce noise, any kind of physical discomfort, emotional distractions, alerts from phones and websites, and people interrupting you, the better you'll focus on the task at hand and immediately get more done.

Since it isn't easy to stay laser focused for a long time, there is a popular technique called the Pomodoro Technique that helps you maintain your focus. In this technique, you choose a period of time during which you will have a singular and intense focus on one thing, followed by a scheduled break to refresh your mind and tend to distractions.

For example, you can choose 30 minutes of work followed by 10 minutes of break, and repeat that cycle throughout the day. It doesn't have to be 30 and 10. You can choose the times that work best for you. If you are just starting out, you can even try as little as 10 or 15 minutes of intense focus followed by a 5 minute break. You'll be surprised by how much you can get done in a 15 minute period of intense focus, and it isn't too difficult to start by focusing 15 minutes at a time.

4. Bigger picture focus for dramatic productivity boost

Whenever top CEOs are surveyed about how they approach productivity, they often answer that they do less work. They identify less fruitful tasks and simply remove those from their schedule.

For example, out of ten things you have on your to-do list now, probably two or three will pay the highest dividends and the others will be much less effective at getting you closer to your goals. The trick is to identify the tasks on your to-do list with the most and least potential and remove the low-potential tasks.

You may immediately gain more time to work on the high-potential tasks, which will allow you to execute those tasks better, making them even more beneficial.

5. Delegation, outsourcing, and automation

Keep an eye out for inefficient processes in your business and consider whether they could be fixed by doing them differently, hiring outside help, finding software to expedite them, or even having custom software built for you.

If you are just starting and you don't have a big budget for outsourcing or building software, start with a budget as low as $50 per month. That isn't a lot to spend, but you might be surprised by how many extra tasks you can get done if you outsource carefully and intelligently by hiring freelancers on websites like Fiverr.com or UpWork.com. Plus, this will give you practice outsourcing and automating for when your business grows and you have a bigger budget.

6. 3 types of business risk

There are three somewhat different types of risks you face when starting a business:

    1) Product risk

    2) Market risk

    3) Financial risk

Not all businesses have each of these risks. As you move through this section, think about which apply to your situation.

Product risk arises when your product is too expensive, complicated, or difficult to produce, which could prevent it from ever being created. If you can't build your product, you will never launch it. Even if you are able to produce your product initially, it may be too expensive or complicated evolve and improve the product due to the costs that come with complexity.

Some examples of businesses that have high product risk are high-tech companies, companies with complicated software, ones that require significant funds or other challenging prerequisites. Such companies may have to go through extensive fundraising processes, hire developers to create mobile apps or software, or may make the initial product overly complex and not follow the Lean Start-Up methodology of Eric Ries which was outlined in the chapter that covered the top business books.

The second type of risk is market risk. This is the danger that once you launch your product, customers won't buy it and sales will be slow or nonexistent. Innovative products typically have significant market risk. A cleaning or a lawn care business has minimal market because such services have natural demand.

The third type of risk is financial risk. Some businesses have minimal financial risk and some have quite a bit. You have to know your tolerance for risking your money and make sure not to choose a business that requires more money than you are prepared to risk.

7. Reversing the NO mentality

Many entrepreneurs often say things like "if I only had money to start my business" or "I'll wait until I have more free time in three months" or "I don't have an engineer to build my product so I won't start" or many other similar statements. Having this mentality prevents people from starting their businesses. Entrepreneurs find solutions to problems. Want-a-preneurs find excuses, feel sorry for themselves, blame external forces, and let problems derail their businesses.

If you find yourself not starting until some barrier goes away, try to change your mindset or your launch strategy. You must be resourceful and creative to find solutions to problems. There will always be roadblocks and problems.

Problems are a part of the entrepreneur experience, and new ones will arise every day. Embrace them and learn to solve them. Keep in mind that there are often many possible solutions to one problem, and you should try to discover better ways to solve your problems instead of allowing barriers to halt your progress.

8. Your ego

As you start your business and especially if you manage to grow it, many people will praise you and tell you how smart and accomplished you are. As success accelerates, so does praise. As entrepreneurs we start to believe it.

Don't.

Stay humble. What you are doing might be great, but there is always more to learn and ways to improve. This is a much healthier mindset. If you let your ego become too large, you will convince yourself that you are great the way you are, don't need to improve anymore, and that will be the beginning of the end. Instead, keep the attitude that you are always just at the relative beginning and you need to learn more and improve yourself in many ways.

Additionally, your feeling of self-worth should come from within instead of from the empty praise of others. You will get a lot of praise if you are in the 90th percentile in your field. But you can't rest there. There is still a long way to go until you reach the 99th percentile.

9. Dealing with stress

Starting my business was one of the most stressful periods of my life. There was stress from lack of finances, business uncertainty, pressure from family and friends, self-doubt, etc. If you are in the process of starting your business now, believe me, I understand what you are going through. Not only did I go through the same stressful period in my life, but I coach many people who are in your exact situation.

Among many negative things resulting from stress, one especially damaging byproduct for your business is that it forces you to make short-term decisions aimed at making a quick buck in the hope to relieve the stress. This comes at the expense of long-term planning that can set you up for much greater success.

For example, when I started my YouTube channel, I rapidly made many videos hoping that they would get many views and I would make money from ad views. But if I took the time to pause and learn how to make better quality videos, my initial videos would have performed much better long-term. Instead, most of my early videos were low-quality and never got many views. I didn't grow my YouTube channel until I stopped being controlled by stress, stopped chasing short-term wins, and took the time to learn how to make better quality videos.

Remember the saying "haste makes waste." When you start your business, haste is often forced by stress and the seeking of immediate benefits, and usually creates a lot of waste. Be careful of stress having too much influence over your business decisions.

10. Dealing with failure

Albert Einstein once said: "Anyone who has never made a mistake has never tried anything new."

As soon as you step out of your comfort zone, you will begin to fail. See it as a good sign instead of a bad one. Every failure or criticism is either a sign that you are learning or a clue to what you can improve. You can use those clues to unearth blind spots in your business and fix them.

It is also much easier to accept failure or criticism if you don't let your ego become too big. Enlarged egos tend to cause fear of failure which leads to stagnation, lack of innovation, and indecision.

When someone criticizes any of my products or posts negative reviews, it doesn't feel good. But deep down I know that their opinion could be shared by others, and if I listen to them closely, they can give me hints to what I can improve. We can even come to appreciate our critics for caring enough to take the time to voice their concerns.

Many ideas for improvements I've made to this book over the years have come after negative reader feedback or reviews. Bad reviews can be hurtful, but they can also be used to improve our products. Of course, it shouldn't be all about negative reviews. If you find the book helpful, I'd appreciate a positive review.

11. Embracing work

Business can sound exciting, but under all the glamour (is there really any glamour in it?) there is boring and hard work.

It's fun to plan, strategize, and dream about your business. But that does not represent the day-to-day work on your business. The day-to-day contains hard and often monotonous work. Many people hesitate at the prospect of hard work; but if you embrace it, you will give yourself a chance to be much more successful long-term.

12. Visualizing success

While it is important to do more work than dream about your business, visualizing your success can be very helpful. Daydreaming about your success and visualizing success can help you see yourself after having achieved your business goals, and cement that reality in your mind, helping you believe that you *can* achieve it.

Just like athletes visualize themselves hitting the winning shot, you have to visualize yourself being successful. That vision will give you a target to work toward and will draw you like a magnet. Plus, it is fun to daydream.

Chapter 14:
Business Registration

"Rules are not necessarily sacred, principles are."

-Franklin D. Roosevelt

Every county in the world has a different process and laws regarding business registration. Even in the United States, the process is different from state to state. In this chapter, we'll cover business registration at a high level.

Disclaimer: This is not meant as legal advice. Business registration will have legal and accounting implications. It is recommended that you get advice from a lawyer and/or an accountant.

1. Are you required to register your business?

People all over the world conduct business without officially registering a business with their local government. Imagine someone paid you to fix something. Did you conduct business? Yes. Do you need to register as a business for something so minor? Yes and no.

In 99% of all such cases, things go well. But in rare instances, you might break whatever you are fixing even further, break additional things, or even worse, injure yourself or others. Additional unexpected costs might arise and disputes, conflicts, and lawsuits may follow.

Any time you conduct business, you run the unlikely but possible risk of something like this happening. It is important to understand how to protect yourself.

2. What is Liability Protection

In United States, if you register a business and conduct your work through that business, if someone sues your business, they are only suing the business - not you directly. This gives you personal liability protection.

Your business can still get sued, but people suing your business can't go after your personal assets like your car or home. That is one of the biggest benefits of registering a business and conducting your work through that business.

3. How to register your business

Every country has a different business registration process, but most of the time it is as simple as going to your local government's website and finding the option for registering your business. For example, in the United States, every state has a Secretary of State website and each state's Secretary of State website has an option for registering your business, which is as simple as filling out some forms right on their website.

If the process confuses you, you can call them on the phone, visit your city hall in person to ask more questions, or have a lawyer help you with your business registration.

EPILOGUE

Starting a business is confusing, and no one becomes an expert overnight or after reading one book. But after completing this book, you are equipped with skills to plan your business in a practical way to get started with a realistic strategy that you can begin implementing earlier rather than later. You should also have a strong sense of what skills will help you execute better so your business doesn't just get launched, but thrives and gets ahead of competition.

Best of luck in all your business endeavors.

Here are a few additional books that might help you in your entrepreneurship journey:

1) **Marketing Plan Template** - This is the sister book for this book. Every business should have a strong business plan AND a strong marketing plan. A marketing plan is just a part of your overall business plan. Here is a shortened URL:

https://goo.gl/YU7sw6

2) **10 Fundraising Strategies** - Almost all entrepreneurs ask about raising money, and you may be wondering about it too. This book gives you 10+ different strategies to raise money for your business. Here is a shortened URL:

https://goo.gl/3fqmBr

3) **20 Productivity Principles** - This book will help you get more done regardless of what you are working on. The book explores 20 different fields of productivity, each of which can give you strategies to get more done starting today. Here is a shortened URL:

https://goo.gl/m6PZQ1

Here is a full list of my 20+ books:

https://goo.gl/WWBcao

Note: if you are in the UK, after you click on the shortened links, change the .com in the URLs to .co.uk

APPENDIX:
Full Business Plan Example
For A Mobile App Company

NOTE: I used parts of this business plan throughout the chapter where we went through writing each section of a business plan. I added the business plan at the end of the book so you can read it in one piece instead of jumping around.

Business Plan For A Business Planning Mobile App

<u>Executive summary</u>

I am building a full 4-app mobile app series for Android and iPhone that will help people plan their business, and support them as they plan, start, and grow their business.

This is a revolutionary new take on mobile apps where the apps become the business coaches for entrepreneurs and give entrepreneurs the support they need to succeed.

There are four apps in the series. Each app covers one of the biggest challenges for entrepreneurs:

- Business idea stage
- Business planning stage
- Fundraising guide
- Marketing training

The comprehensive scope of the apps positions them to be the dominant mobile apps for entrepreneurs.

<u>Product</u>

These are mobile apps for Android and iOS. There are 4 apps on Android and

4 apps on iOS. The apps help people plan, start, and grow their business.

The reason there are 4 apps on each platform is that each of the 4 apps helps entrepreneurs with a specific stage of starting a business. The 4 apps cover:

1) Business ideas

2) Business planning

3) Fundraising

4) Marketing

Each of the 4 apps helps new businesses in these 4 ways:

1) Software tool to help people plan and save their plans right on the app. People will be able to create small business plans, fundraising plans, and marketing plans on the app.

2) Ability to plan parts of their business with partners and invite their whole team to collaborate via the app.

3) Tutorials to teach the entrepreneurs about the business stage they are in: business ideas, business planning, marketing, and raising money.

4) Live business coaching and advice provided by an expert. Until the app has sufficiently grown and to ensure quality of help, the coaching will be provided via text chat on the app by the founder, Alex Genadinik.

Company progress

- Founded in 2012

- 50-100% growth year over year in first 5 years

- 25% growth last year due to saturation on Android and lack of growth on iOS

- Next year focusing on iOS growth

- Over 1,000,000 cumulative downloads across all apps

- Revenue last year: $125,000 *(Fictitious due to privacy)*

Market research & target market

There is extensive research behind these apps. Until the apps reached 300,000 downloads, I (Alex Genadinik) answered every question asked on the apps. Not everyone asked a question, but many people did. Working with such a large sample set of entrepreneurs gave me an unprecedented view and understanding of the kind of help they need, and the questions they have.

The idea for the app series is based directly on the market research of working with such a high volume of entrepreneurs on their businesses.

Besides business ideas, business planning, marketing and fundraising, entrepreneurs also asked about legal and accounting topics. I decided not to cover those topics directly within those apps. Instead, in the long-term, the apps will refer such clients to legal and accounting firms.

Market size

The full potential for my apps will be reached when they dominate search and recommendation algorithms on both Android and iOS.

By dominating in search, these apps can reach approximately 1,000,000 people per year.

Once the apps are widely recognized, they can get big publicity from industry websites, magazines, and by being featured in the Apple App Store and the Google Play store. That would result in 100,000-300,000 additional downloads per year.

An average download generates $1.00 of revenue, which means that at its peak, these apps will generate $1,100,000 to $1,300,000 per year.

(Reminder: The financial data in this example is fictitious. Actual financial data is private.)

Demographics

- Largely under 35 years old (app users are usually younger)
- 35% US, 10% India, 5% UK, 5% Canada, 5% South Africa, 4% Australia, 4% Malaysia, 3% Indonesia, 29% rest of the world including the developing world.
- Low income
- Low education

- Not married

- No children

- Decreased ability to make in-app purchases with credit card due to being in the developing world where not everyone has online banking. Plus, sites like PayPal don't work with dozens of third world countries.

Psychographics

- Don't necessarily need to start a business, just need to make money one way or another

- Largely low tech businesses

- Typically not the Silicon Valley start-up types

- Under financial stress and pressure

- Low confidence in business, maybe told by others not to do business

- Little family support

- Need a solution fast

- Have limited funds

- Prefer free

Competition

- Other business plan templating apps. My apps are different in that they help entrepreneurs create higher quality business plans by educating entrepreneurs and discouraging an overreliance on templates that fill up the business plan with reused content.

- Gimmicky business plan apps that promise business plans in 5 minutes. Since my apps focus on the quality of the business plan and entrepreneur education, the business plans created with my apps are more effective.

- Pen and paper planners. Apps are more easily portable, offer cloud storage for natural backup, and can be used to plan a business with partners remotely.

- Business card apps, business news apps, productivity apps, and other big budget apps. These apps are not direct competitors, but I compete with them for similar searches in the Apple App Store and Google Play Store.

Marketing plan

The marketing of these apps will be through:

- Mobile app store search

- Publicity and PR (being a guest on the radio, podcasts, and being mentioned by blogs)

- Social sharing from people inviting business partners to help plan on the apps

- My website http://www.problemio.com

- Organic Google search

- My YouTube channel where I promote the apps

- Ads on Facebook, Instagram, AdWords, and YouTube AdWords

Since for most apps, the bulk of downloads comes from Android and Apple app store searches, that is where I will concentrate.

Monetization (revenue streams)

- In-app purchases of content

- In-app subscriptions to coaching

- Up-selling coaching services off the app

- Up-selling my books and online courses

- Selling affiliate products like website hosting for new businesses and legal and accounting services

- Sponsors

NOTE: FICTITIOUS FIGURES (THE TRUE FINANCES OF THIS BUSINESS ARE PRIVATE)

Annual revenue: $125,000

In-app purchases of content	$45,000
In-app subscriptions to coaching	$30,000
Up-selling coaching services off the app	$20,000
Up-selling my books and online courses	$10,000
Services	$10,000
Sponsors	$10,000

Next year's projected revenue: $161,000

In-app purchases of content	$60,000
In-app subscriptions to coaching	$40,000
Up-selling coaching services off the app	$25,000
Up-selling my books and online courses	$12,000
Services	$12,000
Sponsors	$12,000

Unit Economics *(fictitious due to privacy with finances)*

Since the product is a digital product and 99% of my marketing is from free sources, there is no cost of goods or marketing costs. Every download brings in *(fictitious)* $0.10 on average LTV (lifetime value of a customer).

The LTV per customer is on par with other apps. Most apps struggle to make significant money per customer and offset that by focusing on generating large volumes of downloads.

Since an app is a digital good and there is no cost to reproduce it like there is with physical products, any revenue is pure profit.

<u>Extending lifetime customer value (LTV)</u>

- I use a "catalog" model to extend LTV by offering many upsells in the apps. I list all of my 20 books and 100+ online courses so when one person buys one, and they like it, they might buy a few more.

- I offer a subscription service on one of the apps. If a person subscribes for a year, that is 12 times more revenue than from a 1-time purchase. This represents a 1200% increase in revenue. A 2-year subscription represents a 2400% increase in revenue from the same customer and so on.

- I offer long-term off-app business coaching which can generate thousands of dollars with the right client.

- Working on supporting the customers better and having them use the app longer with better design, more useful features, and more benefit to them. Longer engagement boosts monetization from those customers.

- Email collection and marketing

<u>Example of an income statement</u>

Cash Flows In (fictitious):

In-app purchases	$20,000
Coaching sold through the app	$50,000
Ads	$10,000
Product sales through the app	$40,000

Subtotal: $120,000

Cash Flows Out (fictitious):

Outsourcing development	$2,000
Marketing costs	$1,000
Apple developer renewal	$100
Loan interest payment	$1,000
Computer deprecation	$500
Donation	$500

Subtotal: $5,100

Balance sheet:

Profitability (Gross profit, net profit, and operating profit)

Gross profit (income remaining after accounting of good sold) - in the fictitious finances of this business, that would be $123,000 annually since the only product creation cost is design.

Operating profit (subtracts additional costs of your business) - since in my business there are minimal other costs, after taxes on $12,000 (minus cost of design AND marketing AND accounting), I make $65,000.

Net profit - after I pay myself ($50,000 annually) the business profit is $15,000

Profit Margin:

Net profit / revenue: $15,000 / $125,000 = 0.12

Note that if I paid myself less, my business would have been immediately more profitable and with a healthier margin:

Net profit / revenue: $35,000 / $125,000 = 0.28

Net profit / revenue: $65,000/ $125,000 = 0.52

Balance sheet *(fictitious)*

Assets:

Current assets:

Cash in the bank	$50,000
Coaching clients payments owed to me:	$3,000
Total:	$53,000

Fixed assets:

Laptop:	$1,000
Office supplies and furniture:	$1,000
Trademark:	$500
Total:	$2,500

Liabilities: None

Outsourcing I owe: $500

Equity: $55,500 - $500 = $55,000

SWOT Analysis

Strengths: best in app store search, deepest customer understanding, personal care, years of experience improving product, ahead of competition

Weaknesses: limited resources to keep growing and experimenting

Opportunities: more app store domination and brand growth and awareness

Threats: easy barrier to entry; bigger money apps can bump me off

Founding team

This is a single founder business.

Alex Genadinik: 5+ years software engineering, 10+ years marketing, 5+ years product creation, successful entrepreneur.

Previous funding and investor ownership

There is no previous funding. The apps were self-funded and created by Alex Genadinik, who retains 100% ownership.

What I am looking for with this plan

My company is looking to get into a start-up incubator and gain access to software development and app usability experts. That help will take the 4-app series to the next level in terms of quality and help it dominate in the app stores.

www.ingramcontent.com/pod-product-compliance
Lightning Source LLC
Chambersburg PA
CBHW081816200326
41597CB00023B/4271